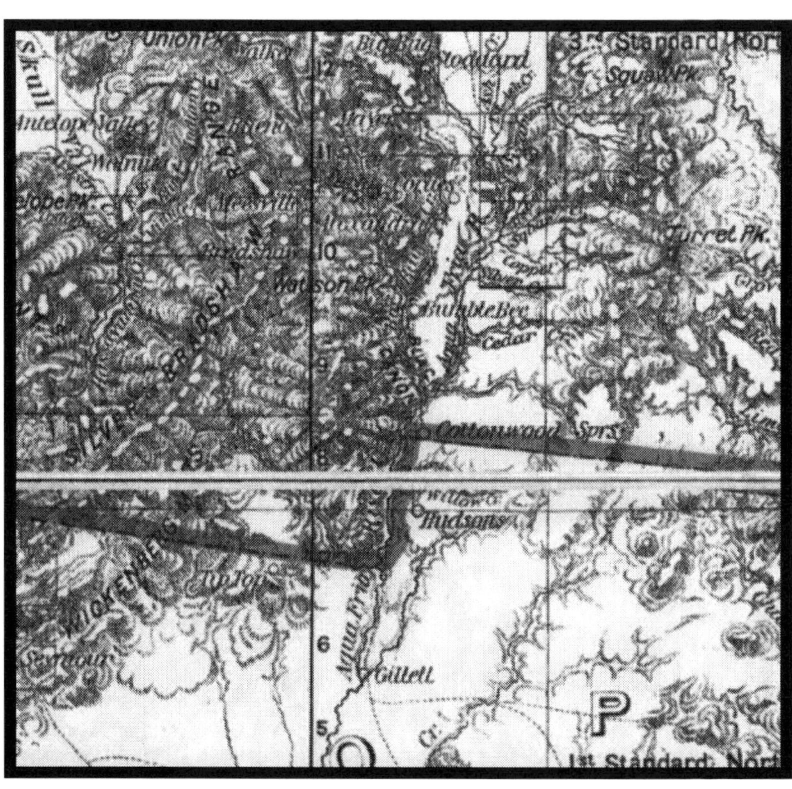

Skull
Union
Big Bug
Stoddard
3 d Standard Nort
Squaw Pk.
Antelope Valley
Walnut
Slope Pk.
Meenville
Buckshin
Watson Cr.
Turret Pk.
Cedar
Cottonwood Sprs.
Willow Cr.
Hudsons
Wickenburg
Tiptop
Agua Fria
Gillett
P
O
1st Standard Nort

Black Canyon
UNDERGROUND

Also by Marcy J. Miller

Crossroads: A Novella

Images of America: New River

Miller's Horse

MARCY J. MILLER

BLACK CANYON UNDERGROUND

Marcy J. Miller is the author of *Images of America: New River, Crossroads: A Novella,* and *Miller's Horse*. She has written for numerous national magazines, maintains a western history blog, and has published fiction, poetry, non-fiction, essays, and columns. She resides in Arizona, her native state, with her husband, too many horses, and just enough dogs and cats.

Black Canyon Underground

Marcy J. Miller

Just West Press
New River, Arizona

For those who love Arizona history in all its gritty glory.

TABLE OF CONTENTS

FOREWORD

I became acquainted with Marcy Miller when we were working together on the Scottsdale Police Department. She is a true daughter of Arizona, born and raised in the Copper State. Her passions are horses and history and she was raised with a genuine love for the people, pioneer culture and history of her native state; this book is a labor of that love.

While Marcy loves telling a good story, and this book is full of them, she is also a stickler for accuracy. That passion for telling what really happened has meant hours upon hours of meticulous research; searching through arcane records, conducting countless interviews and visits to the scenes of the events that she chronicles. It's amazing how much effort she will put into determining exactly where an old stage stop, store or ranch house actually stood; often not where popular histories and common knowledge had folks believing for years.

Another treat is the delightful illustrations that accompany the book, illustrations that were done by Marcy Miller herself. And as with the text, the illustrations are the result of meticulous attention to detail and in keeping with the spirit of the people and events that are depicted.

There are more famous Arizona towns than Black Canyon City, but few that are as steeped in the history of a young territory and continuing drama of a growing state. Marcy Miller makes that history jump off the page. You will become acquainted with heroes, villains and the ordinary people that built and lived their lives in one of Arizona's little known gems; stories that leap off the page and captivate the reader, who will be richer for having had the opportunity to read these tales.

~ John Barto

PREFACE

This isn't the book I first set out to write; or, more accurately, this isn't the book I set out to write first. On the heels of publishing *Images of America: New River,* I was intrigued when Ann Hutchinson suggested I follow up with a book on Black Canyon City. I met with several of the Black Canyon Historical Society's dedicated members and pitched the idea of producing a bound volume of area history. I foresaw a book in the places-and-faces genre, covering facts of mostly local interest.

As I researched, I was soon highjacked by the gripping tales not just of Black Canyon's history, but of Arizona's larger history, that I encountered. I decided I'd follow up the local history with a grittier, bloodier volume anyone who'd grown up in Arizona would relate to. It seemed that underneath each rock I turned over was a body, and each body had a twisted tale all its own. The more I dug, the more I ended up on tangential scavenger hunts. I was obsessed.

Soon the Black Canyon of my book - or, as many of the locals (and I) prefer to call it, Cañon - was but the hub of an imaginary wagon wheel with historic spokes radiating out in every direction, extending far beyond the immediate Black Canyon area. This, then, is the book I originally planned to write second. It isn't all murders and fugitives; I've incorporated stories that come from the Cañon underground literally, such as the history of the Maggie Mine and the healing mud of Mud Springs, and a couple of stories of long-forgotten early characters and their contributions, such as Edward Hildebrand and Leo Leaden.

For months I made a standing open coffee invitation to anyone who wanted to talk history. Black Canyon City residents past and present were beyond generous in opening to me their memory banks and oftentimes their own homes. I rode the old stage road, hiked miles of riverbed, dodged bulls on open range, and sifted manually through microfiched records in Prescott. At night, I spent hours reading old newspaper articles and hunting down vital records. Although I pushed the faces-and-places book back temporarily, I have enough material now to complete it as well - and volumes more.

Black Canyon City is one of the most under-appreciated historical sites in Arizona. It has its own character, a quirky blend of civic involvement and hard-nosed iconoclasm. It's one of the most authentic places I've come to know and love, peopled by unassuming, genuine, capable, pragmatic residents. It's a rugged and gorgeous place, a treasure-trove of characters. I've mined stories much as the early settlers mined minerals. Here, three years in the making, are some of the tales I found most engaging.

For the convenience of the reader, I've opted to add my notes and a brief "aftermath" to each chapter rather than at the end. Those odd little details and follow-up anecdotes were just too interesting not to be included.

If you've shared your knowledge of Cañon's more mainstream history with me and don't find it within, it will be included in the next volume. If you do find a story in this book featuring you, your family, or your collective memories, I hope you'll find I told the story truthfully, accurately, and with respect. That is what I strove to do and I hope I have done so to your satisfaction.

SOME WORDS ON NAMES

History is wiggly. Names are even wigglier. Whether place names or personal names, they're spelled differently throughout the primary sources available. Sometimes a census taker's handwriting left a lot to be desired; other times, the transcriber attempting to type the census records into a searchable online document is simply incompetent. Many times the person being interviewed for a census was illiterate, and they spelled their own names differently - or by necessity left it for the census taker to spell it phonetically - and the same person's name would be transcribed differently in different census years.

Place names were sometimes the victims of bureaucracy. Towns were often given the name of the postmaster, and an eponymous name - one named after a person, such as Gillette, or Goddard - might be the same as that of another post office elsewhere. To avoid confusion, the overseer of post office names might change the name entirely, or just the spelling.

Map-makers might even unintentionally name a place, such as happened with New River, the community south of Cañon. A cartographer noted a new appearance of a river as compared to previous maps and designated it "New River." Map-makers may misspell or misidentify a location; the naming of places is as prone to human error as census writing.

Townspeople, too, changed the names of their towns, or one village might consume another and what was once a series of neighboring towns would be co-opted into one larger town and a single name. And too, people changed their names frequently; my own surname was "Mueller" until World War I, when my German ancestors, in response to anti-German sentiment, anglicized it. It wasn't uncommon for people with distinctly ethnic-sounding names to Americanize them, whether simply to sound American or to make it easier for Americans to spell or pronounce the name. Examples of self name-change occur at times throughout this text, as when Leo Leaden or his family changed their name from "Leyden."

Other times, the west allowed for a certain personal reinvention that comes with a new name - an alias, so to speak. One local character in the 70s was known locally as "Wild Bill," or "Daddy Bill." A fugitive, he assumed the name "Bill Ray Boady" upon fleeing to Arizona to avoid arrest. Bill's real name was Hubert Ray Stidham. He was one of many who chose a new name because of his past. The chapter on the murder of Sgt. Lawrence Broughall is filled with characters who took new names of their own choice due to their criminal lifestyles. Most times, the aliases weren't legal name changes; other times they were. Another individual featured in this book entered the federal witness protection plan (WITSEC) and was relocated to a different state under a different name.

Of course, women's names change due to marriage or divorce. Nicknames sometimes become assumed as formal names, and some individuals are even buried under their nickname; even family members didn't know, or didn't honor, given names. Men who are second- and third-editions - the Juniors and III's of the world - sometimes adopt their middle name to avoid confusion.

When using sources such as newspaper accounts, I encountered numerous misspellings and creative spellings of last names. Sometimes I was able to definitely confirm the correct spelling and tie it to a specific individual; other times, I had a strong hunch or even personal certainty, but couldn't corroborate it. If I use the name without explanation as to whether or not I was in doubt, assume I corroborated it or used the only spelling I encountered along the way. For example, one of the men cited in the chapter on Goddard Station was called "Moodyspaugh" by the newspapers. I strongly believe the last name to be "Mudespaugh" - one of the confirmed locals - but as I could not corroborate my theory, I used "Moodyspaugh" and referenced Mudespaugh. On other occasions, I note in the chapter when I've solved a name mystery.

Many times, a town's name might change as the post office moved; this happened several times throughout Cañon's history. Other times, people would say they're from a more recognizable area than the one they're actually from - for example, someone traveling might tell people they're from "Phoenix" rather than "Paradise Valley" to better communicate the concept of the general area. For these reasons, sometimes I'd find official records where someone from Cañon would say they're from "Rock Springs" on one document, "Black Canyon City" on another, and "Mud Springs" or "Cañon" on yet another. Know that I am writing of the Cañon area in general, and this will at various times include Gillette (sometimes spelled Gillett); Goddard; Mud Springs; Rock Springs; Black Canyon City; and so forth. I prefer to use the name "Cañon" just by personal choice. Since Black Canyon City is neither a chartered city nor an incorporated town, and thus there are no legal city limits, this satisfies my own need for disambiguation.

On some old census records, "Black Canyon" referred to the actual canyon north of what is now Black Canyon City. The confusion this caused was said to have been a driving force in the renaming of the town as "Black Canyon City." Even the name "Cañon" is spelled "Canyon" on some records and "Cañon" on others. You can imagine the joy all these personal and place name changes and creative spellings bring me when trying to digitally search for events and people in the area.

Throw in the name changes that come with marriage, divorce, and so on, and you can imagine the confusion.

So forgive me if I'm occasionally inconsistent with a spelling or a name issue. When I'm transcribing from an official document, I've used the name as written; other times, I may use the name as used by the town or person at the time. Don't get too hung up on names. They're not written in stone … unless they're on a tombstone, and even then, they're often wrong.

Acknowledgments

Countless people contributed to this book, many of whose names I didn't catch but who offered nuggets of information or encouragement. I am sure I've omitted many who deserve, and have, my heartfelt thanks.

Special thanks to:

Debi Allemang, my dear friend who bravely accompanied me on many of the field trips involved in site research for this book.
John Barto, for reading, frequently fact-checking, and providing feedback on the work-in-progress; for his much-appreciated encouragement on this project; and for a kind and eloquent foreword.
David Cannon, for providing expertise and documents relating to the bridge collapse.
Barbara Chatzkel, for encouragement in this project and in the historical mission overall.
Gary Chemas, Robert Cothern, Robert A. Nilles, and members of the Black Canyon Historical Association and the Black Canyon City Chamber of Commerce for contributions that go far beyond the scope of this volume.
Ethelanne Dembow, George Dembow III, and Josh Dembow, for graciously sharing a personal glimpse into the history of the Mud Springs property and the successful family business it spawned.
Barbara Furr, dear friend and companion on many adventures, for serving as an *ad hoc* artistic director and providing feedback on illustrations and concepts.
Shareen Goodroad, for great encouragement.

Ann Hutchinson, for suggesting this project and helping bring it to fruition in so many ways - and for her great patience.

Joe Kertesz, dear friend and encourager, for accompanying me on an archival scavenger hunt in dusty old records - and for moral support.

Jimmy and Shirley Longfellow, for kindly giving me a tour of the Maggie Mine property.

Sylvia McDonald, for sharing her memories.

Raeann Pelleggatti, who graciously brought so many people together to share local history and coffee.

Barbara "Babs" Sanders, who guided me on many field trips to historical sites, including exploring the old stage road on horse and ATV, and who became the dearest of friends along the way.

Carmen "Chuck" Torrie, for sharing his first-hand account of being a first responder at the bridge collapse.

Nora Jean's Koffee Kitchen for their excellent coffee and an inviting place to meet others as I researched this material.

Yavapai County Recorder's Office and staff for assistance in researching official documents.

Chapter 1

Missions of Deviltry

Conflict on the Black Canyon Stagecoach Road

"Pronto! Pronto!" The yells of three Mexican highwaymen broke the darkness of the late-November night. The southbound stage to Phoenix rolled up the hill toward them. They approached both sides of the halted coach on foot. The first one to reach it immediately began shooting at the passenger, William "Billy" Thomas, Johnny Bostwick's partner in a mine at Tip-Top. Billy Thomas didn't stand a chance. The shots were fired at such close range the powder burned Thomas's coat as the bullets struck him. Another outlaw began to shoot at Thomas from the other side, sending a few bullets in the direction of the driver, William C. Ayers. The third robber, speaking English, gave orders to Ayers as Thomas was under attack.

It was about 8:30 p.m. on November 27, 1879, and the stage had but two miles to go to reach Gillette, where the next stage stop offered a brief respite from their travel. The bandits had lain in wait at the steep Black Canyon Hill on a notoriously dangerous stretch of narrow, treacherous road. After firing several shots, none of which struck driver Ayers, the second robber - a man with a hairy and dark mole on his chin, so distinct it was visible in the scant light - attacked the critically-wounded Thomas with a long knife or perhaps, Ayers said, a bayonet. He stabbed Thomas in the chest and stomach until the helpless man collapsed on the stagecoach floor. The attackers then turned to Ayers, climbing to the driver's box atop the coach where he sat. They took the mailbag on board and ordered Ayers to give them his passenger's trunk, stowed in the boot of the coach.

Although brutally wounded, Thomas managed to open the door of the coach. He fell face down in the dirt. Struggling for survival he tried to crawl away, but the three Mexicans set upon him again. By some accounts, Ayers successfully convinced them to leave the injured man alone. When he asked them why they'd attacked Thomas so viciously, one replied, *"Este hombre es no bueno"* - "This man is no good." They frisked Thomas, taking his cash and three newly-repaired watches he'd just retrieved from Thomas J. Morgan's jewelry shop in Prescott.

The highwaymen - such robbers were often called "road agents" at the time - ordered Ayers to unhitch the team of good-looking bays. Each horse was branded with a distinctive isosceles triangle on the left hip. During the unhitching, one of the agitated horses broke free and fled into the night. The Mexicans took the other three, each scrambling bareback onto a horse, and rode back towards Prescott.

The driver, Ayers, tried to make Bill Thomas comfortable, rendering what meager aid he could to the dying man. He then started out on foot toward Gillette. Midway, he located the escaped horse and was able to ride the remainder of the distance. He obtained a fresh team of horses at Gillette and returned to the site to retrieve the stagecoach he'd abandoned.Thomas, left to die in the desert just miles from the mine he owned in Tip-Top, did not survive his wounds. The Prescott newspaper, the *Weekly Arizona Miner,* called the incident a "mission of deviltry" and reported that "several parties have left Prescott in pursuit of the tan-colored boys who committed this daring robbery on the public highway, and woe be unto the rascals if they are overtaken."

The incident was remarkable for its brutality. Although stagecoach robberies were relatively commonplace, few were bloody. Unsurprisingly, people quickly began to doubt that mere robbery was the motive. It was soon conjectured that the robbers had mistaken Thomas for the territorial governor, the famed explorer and former territorial governor, General John C. Fremont. Not long before the attack, Fremont had traveled by coach on the same stretch of road. Perhaps he was the target of an assassination attempt disguised as a robbery.

The day after the attack, the Arizona *Weekly Republican* concluded, "The opinion that murder was their chief design is strengthened on considering the conduct of the highwaymen who almost before uttering a syllable, and before a show of resistance had been made, fired such a murderous volley into an unresisting victim." Citizens of the territory responded with outrage and a large manhunt, but the trail was already cold. In January, a famously effective investigator with experience as both a lawman and a Wells Fargo detective, Deputy U.S. Marshal Robert H. Paul, located a Mexican with a hairy mole on his chin in Davidson Canyon south of Tucson. The teenage suspect, Demetrio Dominguez, carried a watch that Paul determined was one of Bill Thomas's three watches. Marshal Paul promptly arrested Dominguez.

The young murderer was initially escorted to Prescott to face charges. Officials soon realized the incident had occurred just south of the Yavapai line in Maricopa County, a jurisdictional issue that routinely plagued territorial law enforcement officers. They transferred Dominguez to Phoenix where, on October 14th, 1880, a grand jury indicted him and the two older men he'd identified as his still-at-large accomplices, Fermin Fimbres and Gumecindo Moraga.

Above: A section of the Old Black Canyon Stage Road just outside of Black Canyon City as it appears today. The rock berm at center of the photo was part of the road structure. (Author's photo)

Dominguez confessed to the robbery but claimed he'd acted out of fear of Fimbres and Moraga, who'd threatened to kill him. He said he'd participated only as far as unhitching the horses from the coach but that it had been Fimbres who shot Thomas. Despite what information Dominguez provided, Fimbres and Moraga were never apprehended. It was believed they'd fled to Sonora.

Territorial justice moved with a swiftness a modern-day victim couldn't imagine. The day after indictment, Dominguez pled not guilty. A jury was summoned and seated consisting of J. S. Byers, A. Corvels, W. Campbell, E. A. Copeland, William Grear, T. Gregory, M. P. Griffin, N. Herrick, J. Irvine, C. L.

Above: Deputy U. S. Marshal Robert H. Paul, a lawman through and through.

Jones, G. H. Kelly, George Marlar, William Osborn, H. R. Patrick, J. T. Priest, Thomas Rogers, W. J. Scott, W. Seares, J. B. Smith, M. A. Tyler, S. F. Webb, F. G. Wentworth, and Dan White. The trial began the following day, October 16th, prosecuted by A. D. Lemon before Judge DeForest Porter.

Despite the efforts of defense attorneys Frank Cox and J. B. Campbell, two days later Dominguez was found guilty and sentenced to be hanged until dead.

In the few weeks before his sentence was to be carried out, Dominguez whiled his time in jail writing letters, asking help to escape his fate. According to contemporary newspapers, his letters were never mailed. Dominguez also wrote out a full confession in Spanish. The *Arizona Republic* printed a translation of the confession. It ended with the statement, "Gentlemen: I did commit the crime. It is a bad example. I was seduced by those bad men and now I repent of the bad example I have given to the world. I want to be pardoned of this wrong and bad example I have set and want you to believe that I have repented of all my crimes and bad acts. I offer my life as a ransom. I have no more to say."

It was too late for Dominguez, and he would indeed have little more to say. At one p.m. on November 26th, 1880, Demetrio Dominguez was conveyed by carriage to the gallows erected in the Phoenix courtyard. Twenty-five men accompanied the procession to guard against interference by his potential allies, but the heavy guard was unnecessary. No one attempted to save young Dominguez. The next day, the *Arizona Daily Star* described the execution: "After the reading of the death warrant he was asked if he had anything to say. He spoke but a few words, after which he was strapped, the black cap put over his head, the rope adjusted and the trap sprung. His grave was dug within fifty feet of the gallows, and after hanging the time required by law was cut down and buried." The alliteration-loving *Arizona Republic* headlined the story, "HUNG: Demetrio Dominguez Dangles Downward."

Demetrio Dominguez was but seventeen years old. He accomplished little in his short and violent life, but he did make local history: his execution was the first legal hanging in Maricopa County. Lynch mobs had carried out at least four other extrajudicial hangings, and the *Arizona Daily Star* noted that eleven other "rough characters" in the county likely met their end at the business end of a rope.

Above: Isidor Elkan Solomon, Arizona pioneer and founder of Solomonville. Photo credit: J. Connors, "Who's Who in Arizona," 1913.

Dominguez was given a pauper's burial in the early city cemetery in downtown Phoenix between Fifth Avenue and Seventh Avenue. His mortal remains wouldn't long rest in peace. When citizens decided the ill-kept cemetery near the train station was unsightly to arriving passengers to the newly-incorporated city, they decided to dig up the dead and move them to a new location. The proud citizens arranged for paupers to be buried in a mass grave at what is now called the City Loosley Cemetery.

A Double Robbery

Not even a mile north of the site of the William Thomas murder, one of the better-known stagecoach robberies in the Cañon area occurred. Thanks to either the fickle memory or intentionally colorful retelling - or most likely a combination of both - of one of the victims involved, the story has been mis-told many times in papers and books. Like a game of "operator," final versions of the account barely resemble the actual incident. In some historical documents, the robbery is counted double, for years later when passenger and victim Isidor Elkan Solomon told the tale, he said it happened two years earlier and in an entirely different month than the actual date. In 1923, Solomon was interviewed by State Historian Major George H. Kelly about the event. He told Kelly the event happened in February, 1880. In actuality, it occurred on Saturday night, August 26, 1882. To compound the misinformation about the event, the *Arizona Republic* headlined the 1923 interview, "Major Kelly Relates How He Bargained with Robbers to Save His Watch." Major Kelly was simply the transcriber and interviewer and had nothing to do with the actual event.

As Solomon told it, at the time of the robbery he was president of Solomon, Wickersham & Co., a company that operated as merchants and "forwarding agents" in Bowie. As would be expected of such a company, the firm did a substantial amount of business with the U.S. government and Solomon had just collected nearly $2,000 in government checks while in Prescott.

Solomon said the stage left Prescott at two p.m. Inside the coach with him were two men: an unidentified doctor, and Captain Charles G. Gordon of the Sixth Cavalry. The cavalryman knew he was on a dangerous stretch of road. So common were robberies that seasoned travelers cautioned their fellow passengers they'd likely be robbed. Solomon said Gordon had done exactly that, and warned Solomon he should put anything valuable in his boots. Solomon, no stranger to travel on the territorial roads, wasn't worried. He'd planned around that contingency and decided to carry just $50 in cash for traveling expenses, the rest in checks. Solomon suggested that Gordon himself, having more money with him, should take his own advice. Solomon described to historian Kelly how Gordon became nervous as the stage approached the steep hill at which robberies were so easy. The harness animals were always tired as they climbed the upgrade, and the terrain made diverting impossible. Gordon decided to climb onto the driver's box alongside the driver.

As feared, two highwaymen, their faces masked, stopped the stage at gunpoint about an hour later. In a scene that's now a B-western cliche, the men called out, "Throw up your hands." The compliant passengers didn't resist when the robbers rifled through their pockets, removing their watches and cash. The captain had been apprehensive for good reason: he was quickly relieved of nearly $300 in cash, while the doctor gave up less than $10. Solomon coughed up his cash and his valuable watch. The robbers then took the precious Wells Fargo box from the driver's box and began sifting through it.

The robbers were in for a productive night. Midway through the robbery, another stagecoach, this one northbound to Prescott, approached. Considerably more crowded, it carried five passengers in addition to the driver. Solomon said they included a U.S. Marshal he described as "one of the bravest men of the U.S. marshal's force in Arizona at that time," Dick Nagle, as well as three more cavalrymen and yet another doctor. With the second coach's arrival, the robbers bagged more cash and each of the mens' watches. A man's pocket watch was, at the time, often the most valuable item he carried. Clad in gold or silver, they were sometimes ostentatiously engraved and personalized. Although his own open-faced watch was valuable, commensurate with his position as president of a thriving company, Solomon told the robbers it was worth little to anyone but himself and asked if they would be so kind as to give it back. He suspected he might have been recognized by one of the robbers, as the man not only returned it but — when Solomon pointed out how much money they'd gotten from the Captain — gave back Gordon's watch as well.

At this point, seeing the highwaymen to be reasonable pushovers, Deputy Marshal Nagle began to plead his own case, according to Solomon's dubious account. He said his watch had been given to him when he finished his service as chief of police in Tombstone and that it was inscribed with his name and the names of the Tombstone officials who presented it to him. He promised the robbers he'd leave $100 for them any place they designated if they'd let him keep the watch. The frustrated robbers told him he could have his "confounded watch" and returned it.

Solomon, capable negotiator that he was in his version of the incident, wasn't done. In his interview he claimed to have said, "Boys, you have been very nice to my friends. I would like for you to give me enough money to get my supper and a drink." Saying, "Help yourself," the robbers held out a handful of silver dollars. Solomon took seven or eight dollars. The robbers' generosity became a popular legend of the old stage road with the leader of the gang himself accruing locally-given nicknames.

The newspaper accounts of the robbery, written in the days and weeks following the incident, do not bear out most of Solomon's detailed story. The German-born Solomon, at the time the treasurer of Graham County - and the namesake of Solomonville, then the capital of that county - was yet another of the many westerners who had inarguably interesting lives and thrilling experiences, yet chose to embellish them. Solomon's companion on the stage was indeed Captain Charles G. Gordon, but no doctor accompanied them. The most accurate account of the event that I have been able to assemble follows.

"Double Stage Robbery," the September 1, 1882 Prescott *Weekly Arizona Miner* article read. "Two Men Rob the Express and Passengers on the Black Canyon Road." The first coach was "Stewart's Black Canyon stage," a line run by well-known stage man James Stewart, who served as general superintendent of the Arizona Stage Company until retiring in August, 1886. Instead of leaving in the afternoon as Solomon later told, it left Prescott at 8:30 on Saturday morning, August 26, 1882. By nine-thirty that night, the coach was about three miles north of Gillett, between half or three-quarters of a mile from where Billy Thomas was murdered nearly three years earlier. The paper described the robbers as "the knights of the road," and said they "appeared to be experts at the business," rather than the laughable pushovers Solomon recalled. The robbers "examined the condition of [the passengers'] finances, relieving them of the burden of whatever change they had about them." As the outlaws rifled through the express box, another stage did indeed approach. The paper listed the passengers of the second stage as Prescott Doctor F. K. Ainsworth, Tom Wilson, Charles Hurley, G. H. Mandeville, and J. H. Kirk. The newspaper account mentioned nothing of Dick Neagle, nor did it list a doctor among the occupants of the first coach.

The witnesses described the robbers as, "one man about 5 feet 8 inches high, slight built with square shoulders, dressed in dark clothes and hat, armed with repeating rifle and revolver. The other about same height but a little stouter built, had chin whiskers, apparently a little gray. Had on two belts with two six shooters and a repeating rifle."

The newspaper indicated that the doctor, Frank K. Ainsworth, lost $110, "fifty of which he was bringing up as a matter of accommodation for G. W. Curtis, of Gillett." Because the stage carried the express box, Wells, Fargo & Co. offered a standing $300 reward for the robbers' capture. The reward was enhanced by Territorial Governor Frederick A. Tritle's bonus of $300 for each robber convicted, and the Yavapai County reward of $600. Any lawman or bounty hunter bringing in the two suspects and seeing them successfully prosecuted stood to gain $1,800 - a significant amount at the time.

Despite Solomon's many inaccuracies, Deputy U.S. Marshal Neagle was in fact a one-time Tombstone Chief of Police. However, his name was David Neagle, not Dick (and spelled "Neagle," not "Nagle" as the Arizona papers generally spelled it) nor was he yet a Deputy U.S. Marshal. Neagle served as a Cochise County Deputy Sheriff under Sheriff John Behan in 1881. In mid-September of that year, he accompanied Wyatt

Earp, Deputy Sheriff Billy Breakenridge, and other notables in apprehending Frank Stilwell and Pete Spence for stagecoach robbery. That December, after Virgil Earp was ambushed and his left arm badly injured, Neagle succeeded him as Tombstone's town marshal. By January, 1882, Neagle was officially appointed as Tombstone's Police Chief, quickly establishing himself as a popular and competent chief after what the papers described as "the Earp imbroglio." The newspapers - particularly the *Tombstone Epitaph* - fawned slavishly over him, but political favor being fickle, he quickly fell from grace. As had been anticipated, Neagle ran for Cochise County Sheriff that fall, but was defeated. Mid-campaign, the October 10, 1882 Tucson *Arizona Daily Star* carried the short and cryptic opinion, "Nagle of Cochise is a good fellow, but a thoroughbred never enters for a scrub race," while the *Epitaph* was far less generous. The October 28, 1882 *Epitaph* ran a lengthy column citing Neagle's most egregious transgressions, summing it up with, "'Vote for a man who will guard your rights, protect your interests and whom neither land sharks nor ringsters can control or intimidate.' But it won't be for Neagle, for if you are not of his clique neither he nor his officers will protect your life nor property." Clearly Neagle was still Tombstone's Chief of Police at the time, and thus was so employed during the Solomon - Gordon robbery on Black Canyon Hill. As such, despite Solomon's detailed account of Neagle's bartering for his watch, he could not have already received an engraved watch bearing the names of his colleagues and town councilmen to commemorate his retirement. If the *Epitaph* editors' sentiments truly reflected those of the townspeople, Neagle never received that affectionately-inscribed watch at all.

Given Solomon's affinity for creative remembrances, his entire account of the stagecoach robbery - other than those few facts corroborated by accounts of the papers of the time - should be discounted. When the robbery occurred, he was in office as Graham County treasurer, the county seat then being the town named after him, Solomonville. I hope his official accounting was considerably more accurate than his memory.

David Neagle, a wiry 5'7" freckle-faced red-head with eyes described as "steely blue," went on to serve as a U.S. Deputy Marshal in 1886 and to even greater infamy. On August 14, 1889, as part of his service in the U.S. Marshal's department, he was appointed by the U.S. Attorney General to act as bodyguard for Supreme Court Justice Stephen J. Field. While he and Judge Field had breakfast at a railroad depot in Lathrop, California, David S. Terry, a former judge with a long-time grudge against both men approached and slapped Field's face. Neagle responded by shooting Terry in the chest, killing him at the scene. Neagle was arrested by the local constable and, despite stating he was merely doing his duty, was charged with murder. Judge Field was also arrested, but promptly released, while Neagle was held in custody.

Judge Field had once charged both Terry and his wife for contempt of court, and it was Neagle who had been present and had arrested the couple. At the time of the shooting, the Tombstone *Epitaph* - apparently having forgiven Neagle his many faults as local lawman - called him "a man of undisputed courage" who had "once killed a Mexican desperado who'd resisted arrest." Neagle was released after several days in jail and was found by the U.S. Supreme Court to have been acting under the authority of the law when he shot Terry, establishing case law (*In re Neagle*) expanding the enforcement powers of U.S. Marshals. Ironically, Judge Terry had previously survived a duel with another irascible gentleman.

Above: Judge David S. Terry

By 1893, Neagle was working for Southern Pacific Railroad in varying positions of security work, serving as bodyguard and security agent - basically, a hired gun whose reputation as a gunfighter had preceded him. Neagle's name continued to make papers, though. In the summer of 1896, he ran across the editor of the *San Francisco Star,* J. H. Barry, and asked if he was responsible for a particularly unflattering article about him published in the wake of the Terry shooting. When Barry replied in the affirmative, Neagle spat repeatedly in his face. Barry, not unreasonably, attempted to strike him at which point Neagle, his hand threateningly placed against his hip pocket, challenged Barry to "fill your hand." The editor demurred from fighting, saying he was unarmed, and with the assistance of others in the room the men were separated. After yet another incident that month, Neagle was again charged with assault, at which time he was referred to by the prosecutor as a "hired ruffian."

Neagle's long-standing feud with none other than Wyatt Earp himself simmered to a head after the latter incident, and Earp publicly called him out for having made the statement that Neagle had been responsible for running Earp out of Tombstone. At a confrontation in Napa, California, in 1896, Neagle extended his hand to Earp and the men shook as Neagle walked back his alleged remarks about Earp. Earp accepted the apology. The aforementioned 1882 editorial in the *Epitaph,* though, claimed that as Tombstone's Chief of Police Neagle had refused to assist Sheriff Behan in pursuing the Earps after they fled town, and wrote, " … yet he has since had the effrontery to claim the credit of having driven them from the country."

I suspect if hot-tempered and quick-triggered Neagle, by then well known within the territory, had been on the stage from Prescott in August, 1882, he would not have been a passive and compliant passenger when the stage was robbed. As a sworn peace officer at the time it's improbable an experienced lawman wouldn't have taken action, and his name would certainly have appeared in the newspaper accounts of the event. Too, Solomon described Neagle as being a Deputy U.S. Marshal at the time, although Neagle didn't join that agency until years later. Solomon likely added Neagle to the tale to further romanticize what was already an interesting enough story to stand on its own facts and merits. Like the unfortunate Jack Swilling, Solomon appeared prone to glory-telling even when there was little reason to embellish his endeavors and ordeals.

Such was the small world that was Arizona territory; even after moving onto other states and jobs, the cast of characters continued to encounter each other. At some point they all seemed to pass through Cañon, sometimes under remarkable (and other times fictitious) circumstances.

The McClintock Affair

On November 4, 1882, not even three months after the Solomon - Gordon stagecoach robbery, another occurrence on the Black Canyon Road confused and alarmed reporters. The November 11, 1882 *Yuma Sentinel* reported it grimly (I've faithfully reproduced the paper's spelling errors):

Phonix, A.T., Nov. 4. - In shooting affairs last night between two stage drivers, on the Black Canyon road, Peter Connolly was wounded and Jim McClintock mortally wounded, by Joe Caulson, station agent at Gillette. Some of the passengers had narrow escapes during the fusilate.

The Tucson *Arizona Weekly Citizen,* fifteen days after the event, reported that "Jim McClintock, the stage driver who was shot by Agent Coulson at Gillette a few days ago, is now on a fair road to recovery." Apparently Jim McClintock was one tough fellow to survive his mortal wounds. McClintock, as it turns out, wasn't actually resurrected. What actually occurred was far less lethal but far more amusing. The papers, then as now in a hurry to get news into print by deadline, were prone to error and as the Solomon affair illustrates, eyewitnesses and participants weren't always credible. Several varying accounts appeared over the years. The truth died with the stagecoach men themselves, but as Jim McClintock later told it, the story went something like this:

A stagecoach southbound from Prescott stopped at the change station in Bumblebee on the way to Gillette. While there, a stage driver named Jim Wagner had an argument with Pete Connolly, a station hand who tended the livestock. During an exchange of gunshots, Pete went uninjured but Jim Wagner took a bullet in the thigh and, understandably, was unable to proceed. Jim McClintock took the reins of the coach from that point forward and drove it on to Gillette. The passengers, some of whom were working girls on their way to provide physical comfort to the miners at Tip-Top, were in for an even more eventful night. On that cold November night the stage arrived at Gillette at about midnight. The stage delayed due to the conflict in Bumblebee, the soiled doves could find no ride onward to Tip-Top that night, nor did they have other options for accommodations. McClintock asked the Gillette stage agent, Joe Coulson, if he would put the girls up for the night. Coulson, by one account unwilling to aid such women of ill repute, refused to shelter them and McClintock, angry over the stage agent's unsympathetic attitude, told Coulson anyone "who would refuse to take a dog in on a night like that deserved to be shot." Coulson was not persuaded.

McClintock headed downhill to where the coach waited, the team of horses secured only by the reins tied to the coach. Midway up he realized he'd lost his "way pouch" - pocketbook containing his trip documents - on his walk. McClintock checked his overcoat pockets as he climbed up the hill to the station. Coulson, seeing him searching his pockets, thought McClintock was going for a gun and began to shoot. McClintock tried to find his own gun at that point to return fire but was unable to retrieve it through the heavy coat he wore. He felt the bullets striking his coat but by the time Coulson had emptied out his revolver, McClintock was still uninjured.

McClintock returned to where he'd parked the coach only to find it gone. The team of horses, spooked by the gunfire, had bolted. They galloped south on the stage road, crossing the Agua Fria, with McClintock on foot in their wake. As he reached the river bottom, he found the first of the passengers who'd either been flung from the coach or who had bailed out. Continuing to walk, he found the rest. The horses continued onward the entire twelve mile distance to the next change station, Hall's station in New River, where George Hall greeted the exhausted team. Hall took the team and coach back up the road to retrieve the driver and passengers.

Many years later, McClintock happened to meet with a man by the same last name - former Rough Rider, Army surveyor, and Phoenix Postmaster, Colonel James H. McClintock. The popular and highly-respected colonel had been teased by friends who'd read about the affray in a nostalgia section of the 1907 newspaper and wrongly assumed the good colonel had been a stagecoach driver in his youth. Colonel McClintock tracked down former stagecoach driver Jim McClintock, and Jim told the colonel the story above. The driver said that after the incident, he hung up his bullet-ridden overcoat, saying he'd never wear it again. He put the gun belt with it, saying the gun wasn't any good to him either, so he just left it with the coat. He said he'd never worn a gun again. Varied versions of the story were printed not only in the early newspapers but in books and papers over the years.

As for the seemingly inhospitable stage agent Joseph W. "Joe" Coulson, in the fall of 1888 - at about 50 years old - he married a woman named Mary Tracey, much to the surprise of his friends who called him a "sly dog" and regretted they weren't able to give him the grand reception he deserved that "would have shook the leaves off the cottonwood trees and made the coyotes howl for joy." The September 19, 1888 Prescott *Weekly Journal Miner* wished them well: "May they live long and prosper is the sincere wish of their many friends." By December that year, Mary had apparently convinced her husband to move to the city. Coulson sold his hotel and station at Gillette to a man named Evans and moved to Phoenix to start a poultry farm. The Prescott *Weekly Journal-Miner* wrote that B. C. Williams, of Tip-Top, was to manage the old Coulson station, predicting it would maintain its success in Williams' hands.

By 1895, Coulson appeared in the Phoenix directory as a harness maker. In 1906, he suffered a serious fall at his home at 448 W. Washington while repairing an awning at his home. Coulson lost consciousness for several hours, not awakening until midnight and scaring his friends who feared he wouldn't survive. But survive he did, appearing in regular ads in the paper for Doan's Kidney Pills. "For some time I was about laid up with my back," his testimonial read, "There was a dull, nagging pain across my loins and kidneys which bothered me almost constantly. About two years ago I had a fall which injured my back and I was unconscious for many hours. This was the beginning of my trouble and I knew that my kidneys were affected. The use of three boxes of Doan's Kidney Pills brought me relief and I have had no trouble to speak of since. I am a strong supporter of Doan's Kidney Pills."

Aftermath and Author's Notes

John C. Fremont, frontiersman, cavalry officer, Arizona territorial governor, and failed candidate for president, died on July 13, 1890. Known as much for his rash decisions as for his willingness to initiate new adventures, his Arizona governorship was little more than a sinecure.

James Harvey "Jim" McClintock, a captain of the Rough Riders in the Spanish-American War, had the misfortune of being the first Arizonan wounded in Cuba. Generally referred to as "Colonel McClintock," he was a colonel in the Arizona National Guard. McClintock, a longtime postmaster of Phoenix, was widely respected for his expertise on Arizona's history and native people. A prolific writer and public servant, he died in May, 1934, in the National Soldiers' Home in Sawtelle, California.

David B. Neagle died at age 78 in Oakland, California, on November 28, 1925 after an illustrious career worthy of its own book. The Boston-born lawman was survived by his wife, Bertha, and his daughter, Mrs. Winifred Halter, and his son, Albert V. Neagle. Neagle's services were "strictly private," a fitting end for a somber man. Neagle's widow died just shy of two years after his death, on November 14, 1927.

Isidor Elkan Solomon, founder of Solomonville, Graham County treasurer, influential merchant, and teller of tall tales, went on to a successful career in banking. By 1904, he was vice president of the Gila Valley Bank, by 1908 becoming vice president of the newly-reorganized Bank of Safford.

In January, 1905, Isidor's brother, Adolph, committed suicide at the Jones Hotel in Safford despite Isidor's efforts to help him through his despair. Isidor and a mutual friend stayed at Adolph's side when they recognized he was suicidal. Upon asking him how he felt, Adolph replied that he'd never felt better in his life. Adolph excused himself to get something from storage in the hotel yard, and within minutes, his two guardians heard the fatal gunshot. He died in 1930. He's buried in Hollywood Forever Cemetery in Hollywood, California.

Sources for this chapter include newspaper archives originally reporting the events I've chronicled, with emphasis on

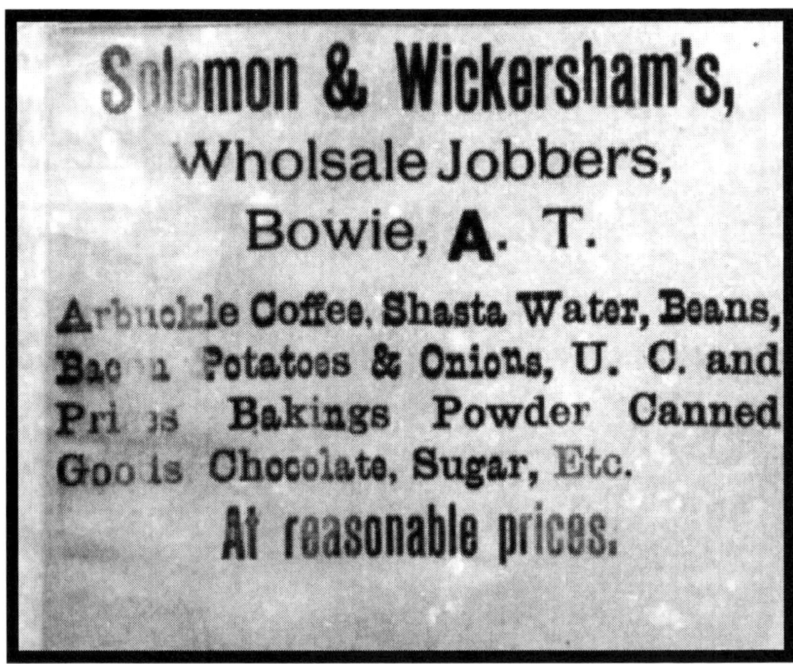

Above: Newspaper ad for I. E. Solomon's firm, 1899.

The Arizona Republic, the *Arizona Daily Star,* the *Prescott Weekly Arizona Miner,* the *Tombstone Epitaph,* and the *Tucson Arizona Weekly Citizen.* I also used official documents to include territorial census reports, military records, and draft registration. Site visits included exploring the old Black Canyon Stagecoach Road on horseback and ATV and hiking the ghost town of Gillett. Babs Sanders generously guided me on many of those expeditions. Mr. David Turk, official archivist for the U.S. Marshal's Service, was kind enough to answer my inquiries about Deputy U.S. Marshal Neagle.

Additional reference materials included (but aren't limited to) the following:

Connors, J. *Who's Who in Arizona.* 1913.

Thrapp, Dan L. *Encyclopedia of Frontier Biography.* Spokane, Washington: The Arthur H. Clark Company, 1990.

Traywick, Ben T. *Historical Documents and Photographs of Tombstone.* Tombstone, Arizona: Red Marie's Bookstore, 1994.

The illustration at the beginning of this chapter is my original woodcut block print depicting a Concord stagecoach.

Chapter 2

Jack of Hearts

Swilling's Cañon Years

Pack-driver and prospector Thomas Mallon had a reputation for trouble. By the time he arrived at Jack Swilling's ranch on the banks of the Agua Fria, others on the place knew he'd killed a man that spring. He'd been in the Globe district that spring when he shot a man whom the papers referred to simply as "Brannaman" sometime around March 1, 1877. The victim was one of the territory's pioneers, John M. Branaman, who ran a small silver mill along Pinal Creek in Globe City - the name, then, for what is now simply called "Globe." According to the March 10, 1877 *Tucson Citizen*, "John M. Branaman died February 15th of inflammation of the brain caused by a wound in the front part of the head rupturing the skull." John's estate was in probate by April, 1877, with Elizabeth R. Branaman serving as estate administratrix.

Over the summer, Mallon's temper flared again. He and a fellow packer, Henry Randall, argued over a pack-saddle at Swilling's place. Since 1875, Swilling's Station was the stagecoach stop in Cañon. Travelers along the Black Canyon route frequently stayed at the Swilling Ranch at the juncture of the Agua Fria and Black Canyon Creek. On July 29th, at about six p.m., Randall - whose name appeared as "Henry Randel" in some newspaper accounts - fatally shot Mallon with a double-barreled shotgun. Mallon died instantly. Randall turned himself in to the sheriff's office in Prescott on August 2nd. The Prescott *Miner* suggested he didn't want to give Randall "any advantage" during the conflict, knowing Randall was already a killer.

Mallon was buried on the Swilling Ranch. His wouldn't be the only body laid to rest there.

One of Arizona Territory's most compelling figures, John "Jack" Swilling spent just a few years in Cañon - living at his ranch there off and on from 1868 to 1877 - but as with all of Swilling's years, they were eventful, productive, and often dark. Swilling, accompanied by his ever-patient wife Trinidad and an array of children, moved around constantly in pursuit of one opportunity after another. He left his mark at each stop. In one settlement he founded once known as "Pumpkinville" he was one of about twenty men present when "Lord" Darrell Duppa suggested the name that would stick: "Phoenix." He was the first Postmaster of Phoenix, the first president of the Maricopa County Democratic Convention, and an energetic (but under-appreciated) visionary.

It was Swilling who recognized the potential of the ancient Hohokam canals that traversed the valley and, in partnership with others, formed irrigation companies using them. From serving as a soldier of the Confederacy, to participating in the 1863 Walker Party that sought gold along the Hassayampa, to land speculation, ranching, farming, and mining, Swilling was part of all the important enterprises of territorial Arizona. He was a politician, an opiate addict, a businessman, a loyal friend, a drinker, a killer, and a blowhard. He was famously generous and - when under the influence of his addiction - infamously wild. In an 1864 letter to an Albuquerque newspaper, one man described Swilling as "… a tall, athletic, bluff, straightforward, frank man, over six feet high, light complected, with a clear, bright eye, and determination written in every lineament on his face. He is a quiet man, but interesting in conversation and is, I judge, a man of warm and generous impulses." That year, Swilling married seventeen-year-old Trinidad Escalante.

In 1865, Swilling filed a claim in Maricopa County to a mine in Black Canyon district. His claim read, "I claim 300 feet on either side of this vein, and as far north and south as my Winchester will shoot."

Above: The ruins of the Swilling ranch house in Black Canyon City.

By the time he built his modest stone home in Cañon, Swilling was already in poor health. Years of physical pain from an altercation in 1854 that left him with a fractured skull and a bullet lodged in his side resulted in an addiction to morphine and alcohol. The sole known photograph of him shows a man gaunt from addiction, his rifle slung over his shoulder to give the effect of being a gunman, an Indian child beside him. That child,

Gavilan, along with a girl named Mariana, was one of Jack and Trinidad's two adopted Apache children. Swilling was a husband to two, a father to many, and a benefactor to many more. It was as a father one of his many sadnesses occurred. While living in Cañon, he and Trinidad lost their eight-year-old daughter, Matilda, on October 19, 1875. Barely a month before, on September 13, Jack's father George Swilling died in Georgia. (Georgia, incidentally, was also the name of one of Jack and Trinidad's daughters.) The Swillings buried their daughter near their house at the ranch on the Agua Fria. Trinidad - referred to in the paper as Doña Trinney Escalante in Matilda's obituary notice - was expecting another child at the time. The new baby arrived around May, 1876. They named her Matilda Adaline, commemorating their lost child of the previous year.

The August 20, 1876 *Weekly Arizona Miner* posted an article about Jack Swilling being cheated by a man who identified himself as William Little. Jack, by then, was a successful agriculturist at his Cañon ranch. The article, headed "Bad Man," said that Little and a wagon with a two-horse team arrived at the ranch claiming "Mitchell and Gardner" had sent him for a load of watermelons. Swilling gave him the melons and sent him on his way. Swilling had previously sent a wagon to Mitchell and Gardner for repair. After a few days he rode to town to ask about his wagon, only to learn that since the repair was going to be delayed, Mitchell and Gardner had thoughtfully sent Little with a "loaner" wagon for Swilling to use. It wasn't until a week later they'd found the team and wagon at Brooke and Linn's Plaza Feed and Sale stable on Goodwin Street opposite the plaza in Prescott. Little had skipped town. Bad-luck Jack lost not only the wagon load of melons, but had no way to transport the rest of his crop to market. Melons being melons, most of his crop rotted in the heat of August. The same week, the postmaster at Prescott absconded with ten to fifteen thousand dollars of ill-gotten funds. It was a lively time for crooks and scammers in the territory.

During his Cañon years, Swilling was one of the founders of Gillett, the town that serviced the mines at Tip-Top and offered a stage stop for travelers along the Old Black Canyon Stagecoach Road. It was from Gillett that Swilling, accompanied by Thomas Barnum, Andrew Kirby, and George Monroe, left on a mission urged by Trinidad as a diversion intended to save him from himself and the bottle. In March of 1871, Colonel Jacob Snively, one of Swilling's good friends, was killed by Indians a few miles northeast of Wickenburg by a peak called White Picacho. Snively was buried at the scene of his death. Trinidad, playing on Jack's sentimental side as well as his need to be kept occupied, suggested he retrieve Snively's remains and bring them to the ranch for a proper burial. In mid-April, 1878, the recovery party headed for White Picacho.

The four men safely returned by April 25th and buried Snively's remains in the family cemetery near Thomas Mallon and young Matilda. Not long afterward, Jack Swilling and Andrew Kirby were arrested at a saloon in Gillett by Yavapai County Deputy Sheriff H. H. McCall for a stagecoach robbery that occurred on April 19th while the men were in the Wickenburg area. Because U.S. mail was handled, the crime was a federal offense. The descriptions of the three masked robbers matched Swilling, Kirby, and Monroe. Swilling honestly admitted that the descriptions of the road agents loosely matched those of he and his travel companions. His honesty - and his propensity for drunken confession and tall tales - was used against him as evidence. So, too, were statements made by a double-crossing friend named L. G. Taylor.

In June, the federal charges were dropped. However, a Deputy U.S. Marshal and Wells Fargo agent named John W. Evans pursued the territorial charges against the men. He clandestinely conveyed them to Yuma where they were jailed not in the famous Yuma Territorial Prison but in the primitive, miserable accommodations at the Yuma County Jail. Despite the later reputation of the Territorial Prison, it was state of the art for its time and spoken of as "the country club on the Colorado" by scornful citizens who felt it too posh. Had Jack Swilling actually been imprisoned post-conviction rather than jailed pre-trial, his fate may have been different. The Territorial Prison, built in 1876, boasted amenities such as a prison hospital, library, exercise yard, and work programs. Instead, in the heat of summer, the already frail Swilling declined dramatically in notoriously hot Yuma.

June 24th brought the arrival of Jack's last-born child. As he suffered in jail, Trinidad gave birth to John William Swilling, Jr. By then Jack Sr. - who'd only weighed a terribly thin 105 pounds prior to his arrest - was rapidly dwindling.

Swilling knew he was but briefly to survive. He wrote heartbreaking letters swearing to his innocence and that of Monroe and Kirby, "as God knows they are innocent." The saddest passage of his letters stated, "This cruel charge has brought me, for the first time in my life, under a jailer's key. My persecutors will remember me. And may God help my poor family through this cold world, is my prayer."

On August 12th, 1878, John "Jack" Swilling died in abject misery at age 58 in Yuma. His reputation forever sullied, separated from his beloved family, his freedom gone, in physical and emotional pain, and knowing death was imminent, Jack's body finally gave out. On October 1, Deputy Marshal Evans telegrammed Kirby that he would soon be released, his claims of innocence having been substantiated. Swilling's partner in the recovery mission, but not in crime, Andrew Kirby was released on October 2nd. Swilling's innocence, too, was clearly established. Deputy Marshal Evans ultimately arrested the three men responsible for the stagecoach robbery for which Jack had been jailed.

Nine days after Kirby's release, the Prescott *Weekly Arizona Miner* carried a passage reading, "Now that Jack Swilling is dead, his wife a widow and his children orphans in poverty and want, all the papers and many of the people are commiserating the fate of the family and mourning the death of the husband and father, whereas during his lifetime and false imprisonment many were offended at the MINER, and cursed its editor for daring to say a word in favor of the innocence of these men. Remarking upon the established innocence and liberation of Kirby, which carries with it that of Monroe, the Sentinel says Jack Swilling was confined with Kirby, but died in jail before his innocence was established. All his property was dissipated in vain efforts to clear himself. To his wife and children there now remain a heritage of poverty, widowhood and orphanage, offset only by the pitiful, mournful proof of their dead one's innocence of the charge on which he was imprisoned."

After his final legal battles, Jack had little left for his wife and surviving children to inherit but his tragedies. On November 10th, 1879, his youngest child, little Matilda Adaline, died in Phoenix. She was just three years and seven months old. Her death was to be one of Trinidad's many losses.

Above: Trinidad Mejia Escalante Swilling Shumaker, Arizona pioneer.

Trinidad and her Children

Jack's devoted wife, Trinidad Mejia Escalante Swilling, deserves more than just passing notice in the annals of Arizona history. Born in Mexico of Spaniard parents, Trinidad was the first non-indigenous woman to settle in the Salt River Valley. She married Jack at just 17 years of age, bearing him seven children: Georgia, Lillie, Elizabeth, Berry, the two dead Matildas, and John Swilling Jr. It was clear Jack loved Trinney, but openly admitted (and regretted) his abuse towards her when he was drinking or taking opiates. Her life was heartbreakingly difficult.

Upon Jack's death, Trinidad moved back to Phoenix, supporting herself as a seamstress. She later remarried, this time to a German barber and saloonkeeper from Yuma named Henry Shumaker. Sadly, Shumaker was also reputed to have abused her. With Henry, Trinidad had three sons: Charles, Robert, and Henry Jr.

The elder Henry Shumaker, apparently having struggled with depression and mental illness, committed suicide by morphine overdose on March 11, 1896, leaving Trinidad to care for her many surviving children alone. His suicide note read, "Please take me to Davis' undertaking parlors. Do not take me home, and save my wife and the babies all trouble. Please make sure not to bury me until I am dead. My life has been a complete failure. Goodbye, wife, babies, and friends. H. Shumaker."

On August 24, 1907, Trinidad suffered another tragedy. Her adult daughter Lillie Swilling, under the assumed name of Josie Bell, had been working as a prostitute in Tucson's red-light district for several years. Whether it was the hardships of the lifestyle, the demons she'd inherited from her father, or the accrued sadness of her life experience, Lillie committed suicide by shooting herself. Lillie, born in Ash Fork in May of 1872, was only 36 years old. An article in the Globe *Arizona Silver Belt* gave a heartbreaking account of her death. It said she'd been drinking at the saloon where she kept a room, then returned to her apartment at 44 Mesilla Street, where she lived with a man named Charles Craig. Craig commented on her state of intoxication and how she would feel the next day, and she replied she didn't care as it was "all over anyway." Craig left the room to make something to eat. Hearing a single shot, he returned to find she'd shot herself in the chest. Charles sought help from a woman across the street, Pearl Howard, but as soon as Pearl returned with him, Lillie let out three long breaths and then died. She was buried in the Tucson City Cemetery.

In 1918, Trinidad's son Charles Shumaker, born the same year of his father's suicide, died in France. He was in the service of the Navy in World War I. Charles was but 22 years old. Just two years later, in 1920, his brother Robert Shumaker died in an accident in Sonora, Mexico.

Both sons of Jack and Trinidad inherited their father's wanderlust and sense of adventure. Their eldest son, Berry Burton Swilling, was born on March 12, 1873. Throughout his life, for reasons entirely his own, he used different birth years on documents, and generally chose to spell his name "Barry."

On his 1896 passport application, Berry used a birthdate of March 12, 1876. He gave his permanent address as Manila, Philippines, and stated his intentions of traveling to Hong Kong, Japan, and China. In 1899, Berry enlisted in the 18th Infantry of the Army and served with K Company in the Philippines. At the time of enlistment, brown-eyed and dark-complected Berry was 5'6 and 1/2" and working as a stenographer.

In 1917, Berry married Elizabeth Menke. He'd lived in San Francisco for several years by then and worked in a clerical position. Around 1921, Barry moved to Texas where he worked as an immigration inspector. On October 20, 1922, he died of what his death certificate described as "acute indigestion" in

Above: Berry Burton Swilling, Jack and Trinidad's oldest son, in his 1896 passport photograph. Although not so gaunt as Jack, the resemblance to his father is clear in his features.

Maverick County, Texas. Berry was buried in Eagle Pass Cemetery.

Berry's death took a tremendous toll on Trinidad's health. She had remained active in pioneer reunions and activities, with newspaper accounts mentioning her regularly in conjunction with such events, but after Berry died, the papers more often mentioned her illnesses. She died of stomach cancer on December 27, 1925 at age 76 and was buried next to the remains of her son, Charles Shumaker, in St. Francis Catholic Cemetery in Phoenix. It is yet one more of the many injustices of Trinidad's life that for decades her grave remained unmarked. It wasn't until 1997 that a headstone was finally placed on her place of rest. According to some newspaper accounts, only Henry F. Shumaker survived her.

John "Johnny" W. Swilling, Jr., was well known around Phoenix. Having a penchant for music and acting Johnny was mentioned in the *Arizona Republic* in the summer of 1897 as "becoming famous as a 'play actor.' He appears every evening at the park theater either as a soldier, sailor, brigand or any other old thing." He spearheaded the development of a drum corps in Phoenix in 1898 to properly celebrate Washington's birthday. A year later, proudly patriotic Johnny no longer had to pretend to be a soldier. He enlisted in the U.S. Army in 1899, leaving for the Philippines on July 27th to fight in the Spanish-American War. The *Republic* remarked, "Johnny Swilling, whose whole life has been spent in this valley and who has had the war fever ever since the trouble with Spain started, enlisted with the boys who left last night and is now on his way to the Philippines." By 1905, the *Arizona Republic* praised him freely, noting that Johnny "served as a non-commissioned officer in the Thirty-fourth Regiment of U.S. Volunteers and is every inch a soldier." In a letter home from the front in March of 1900, Frank Welden, one of Johnny's fellow soldiers from the Thirty-fourth, mentioned Johnny was well and was with the regimental band. Welden's letter gave a glimpse into the hardships under which the men served: "No tongue could describe what we have endured. After leaving Pasig, we marched 400 miles through mud and water. For days and weeks we were in wet clothing, with no chance to dry ourselves, as it rained day and night and we were without shelter. Out of 400 men who left Manila on October 27 but sixty went the entire distance. The rest gave out and had to be left along the road … Nearly all the Phoenix boys got through and are in good shape." Smallpox did take its toll, and troops mourned one popular Phoenix soldier, Frank Holliday, who died at Bigan. Although some references state that one or both of the Swilling boys was a member of the famed Rough Riders Cavalry, neither Berry nor Johnny - nor any man with the surname Swilling - appear on the roster for that particular regiment, officially known as the 1st United States Volunteer Cavalry.

On February 10, 1902, Johnny married a California-born girl, Harriett "Hetty" A. Devilbiss, in a Catholic ceremony in Phoenix. Hetty (who appears as "Henrietta" in some records and "Teresa Henrietta" in others) and Johnny had three children - Cecil, Lucille, and George. Johnny continued to serve in the Yuma National Guard, and in 1905 was elected second lieutenant. As a guard at the Yuma Territorial Prison, in 1908 Johnny worked for none other than the one-time captain of the Arizona Rangers and former officer with the Rough Riders, Tom Rynning, who'd been appointed superintendent of the prison.

However, not all was well on the domestic front, and by 1910 Hetty and the children were living with her parents, Henry and Julia Devilbiss, and several siblings in Los Angeles. The census records indicate she was still married, but clearly she had separated from Johnny. Hetty took work as a stenographer in a doctor's office and eventually remarried. Hetty lived until 1951.

In 1916, 43-year-old Johnny remarried also, this time to 46-year-old New York-born May R. Porter in Phoenix. Johnny continued his musical pursuits, playing in "The Pioneer Band" in Phoenix in 1917. By 1920, in the sad tradition of so many Swilling women, May - not even fifty years old - was widowed. She moved to Los Angeles where, by 1932, May appeared in voter registration as a Republican living at 812 N. Allen Avenue.

Although Jack Swilling lived a tragic life, Trinidad not only shared his hardships and sadnesses but had far more of her own. In addition to the hardships of pioneer life and the particularly unique challenges of her marriage to Jack Swilling, Trinidad buried nine children and two abusive husbands.

History seldom gives pioneer women their due. In 1922, during coverage of the Arizona pioneers gathered at the annual reunion, the *Los Angeles Times* said this of Trinidad: "Especially honored in the gathering will be Mrs. Trinidad Shumaker, a retiring little woman of Mexican ancestry, who has a place in Arizona history through the fact that she is the widow of Jack Swilling, one of the most picturesque of early Arizonans ..." How sad that Trinidad, the first white woman in the valley, who gave birth to ten children in conditions that could be described as crude at best - and lived to grieve nine of them - should be described as nothing more than "a retiring little woman of Mexican ancestry" who married a man of some note and considerable notoriety.

Aftermath and Author's Notes

Jack and Trinidad's stone house in Cañon still stands on the south bank of the Agua Fria, carefully preserved by the landowners. Sadly, although the road was once known as Swilling Road, it no longer bears his name. The graves of Thomas Mallon, Matilda Swilling, and Colonel Jacob Snively are unmarked; according to Trinidad, an Indian who'd worked on the ranch was also buried at the small ranch cemetery. Jack's own remains were never granted the same respect given those of his friend Snively. Barely had he died when his body was planted in Yuma, not far from the jail, even before Trinidad was notified of his death. No one retrieved them and gave him a proper burial. Again, as had happened countless times throughout his life, Jack was denied the same generosity and kindness he'd shown to others. Although local historical researchers have a general idea as to location, there is no gravesite to visit to pay the respects due to him for his many contributions to the fledgling Arizona territory and its people.

There are still traces of ruins in the ghost town of Gillett, also founded by Jack, five miles south of the Swilling's stone house and on the other side of the Agua Fria.

In an interesting side-note, in 1914, Jack Swilling's Winchester rifle was found by famed pioneer Charles B. Genung in the cellar of an abandoned house in Peeple's Valley. Bearing a plate engraved with, "Made Expressly for John Swilling by the Winchester Arms Company," the rifle was claimed by Trinidad Swilling, who lived in Los Angeles at the time.

In 1952, Trinidad's one surviving son, Henry F. Shumaker, collapsed on Main Street in Clarkdale and died. Born in 1888, he was only 64 when he passed away. Although Henry's wife survived him, apparently no children did.

In New River, a distinctive landform called Gavilan Peak has served as a landmark for travelers since at least the 1800s, and likely for native people before that time as well. From the south, the peak appears to be the profile of a prone Indian man's face. From the west, it's a single peak of a singular shape; from the north, it is clearly two sister peaks (and many locals called it "Twin Buttes" or "Twin Peaks" for that reason). The story of how Gavilan Peak was named varies. One version claims it is named after the Indian chief buried at the base who swore his spirit would protect white settlers in the surrounding areas. Others say it is so called for the hawks in the area, as the word "gavilan" means "hawk." I believe Jack Swilling, who was involved in the settling and naming of so many Arizona places, named it for his adopted Apache son, Gavilan Pollero ("chicken hawk"). Jack had passed that landform hundreds of times in his travels.

As for Gavilan himself, he later changed his name to Guillermo and seemingly vanished from written history. The later history of his sister, Mariana (alternately appearing as "Mary Anna" in some documents) is also unknown. Though Jack didn't legally adopt the children - adoption of Indian children being illegal until 1873 - such children could be legally "indentured." This legal process was often used as a means of adoption rather than servitude. According to Albert Bates in his excellent volume on Swilling, Jack signed the indenturement papers on Gavilan in 1871. Bates cites early references stating the two children were given to the Swillings by Pima Indians who had captured them in Cave Creek after a battle with a band of Apaches.

In addition to the daughter Elizabeth whom Jack had with his wife Trinidad, he was survived by a daughter named Elizabeth born to his first wife, Mary Jane. Years before marrying Trinney, Jack had abandoned Mary Jane and baby Elizabeth in Alabama. Mary Jane may have long labored under the belief he was dead. In 1992, when the Salt River Project unveiled an extensive exhibit dedicated to Swilling, over forty of the Swilling family members, many of whom were descendants via his daughter with Mary Jane and those from his Arizona family, met at the event. They're heirs to an incredible family history and the legacy of a fascinating man who was ever at the forefront of some of the territory's seminal events.

Thankfully, the paper trail Jack Swilling left is long and detailed due to his many civic contributions and involvement in so many historical events. I have relied largely on newspaper archives, census records, land records held by the Yavapai County Recorder's Office, site visits, and several books including those cited below. Additionally, the Arizona Salt River Project has an extensive collection of Swilling documents and artifacts.

Bates, Albert R. *Jack Swilling: Arizona's Most Lied About Pioneer.* Tucson, Arizona: Wheatmark, 2008.

Wilson, R. Michael: *Tragic Jack: The True Story of Arizona Pioneer John William Swilling.* Guilford, Connecticut: The Globe Pequot Press, 2007.

Related site visits included Swilling's stone house in Cañon, Gillett ghost town, and Yuma Territorial Prison.

The illustration at the beginning of this chapter is my original linocut block print depicting an Arizona adobe home.

Chapter 3

If That Was a Song I Would Sing it to You

The Goddard Station Murders

No one gave too much thought to the two Mexican men who appeared at Charles Goddard's place that cool Sunday afternoon in 1903. Travelers were commonplace and especially so that time of year: it was the first day of February, and shearing season was in full swing. Herders and shearers swelled the number of people making their way along the dusty stage road through Cañon. Goddard, a 50-year-old merchant and goat rancher, ran a stage stop and sheep shearing station on the south bank of the Agua Fria upriver from Jeff Martin's store. Goddard Station was a popular destination for sheep ranchers who contracted with Goddard to provide shearing services at eight cents per head. Comprised of a house and general store to the west of the stage road with a barn and corral to the east, the site also served as a post office.

The January just five years prior, Goddard - an affluent man in the area for the day, and popular with locals - had 100,000 sheep at his station awaiting shearing. Thirty men were kept at work the 1898 season, each shearing 60 to 70 sheep every day. By 1902, Goddard had installed a patent steam-operated shearing plant at Congress Junction, some miles to the northwest. There, with its fourteen shears, the machine could handle as many as 300 sheep per day, mechanically removing the wool far more rapidly than even the most fast-handed human. Thirty-thousand sheep awaited spring shearing. Charles Goddard anticipated a good season for 1903.

Still in a battle for statehood, Arizona took due pride in its sheep industry and took every opportunity to promote it nationally. Still, some factions fought the sheepmen. By the end of February, over a thousand sheep would be poisoned farther down in the valley near the Arizona Canal by blue vitriol, a copper sulfate, maliciously scattered across the sheep range. The sheep, seeking salt as livestock do, eagerly licked it up and died a miserable death. Those woolies who survived were moved to safety to the north along the Agua Fria.

Like other station keepers along the river, part of Goddard's livelihood depended on providing meals and lodging for the stream of travelers on the Black Canyon Stage Road. Earlier in the day that unforgettable Sunday, Francisco Hernandez, a Mexican sheepherder, had arrived at Goddard's Station from an outfit up north. He was to work for Goddard. Charles' younger brother, Frank, had also arrived that day, coming in from "the east." Frank joined several others staying at the station: his sister-in-law Rosa, Charles' wife; an invalid 32-year-old mining engineer named Milton Turnbull; and Charlie's clerk and foreman, sometime-teamster Frank Cocke.

The two newly-arrived Mexicans, clad in blue overalls and canvas duck coats, chatted up Hernandez outside the station. Arriving at around 3:00 in the afternoon, they had lunch inside, returning to make more conversation. They inquired about the Goddards' habits and the usual routine there at the station. The younger of the two, standing about five foot seven, had a distinctive scar on his face and a darker complexion than his companion. The other was a couple of inches taller and bore the tell-tale pockmarks from smallpox on his face. Around thirty years old, he was a nail-biter. Both men had mustaches. On Friday, they'd been to Prescott, where they'd purchased a couple of Colt revolvers - a .38 and a .41 caliber - from a merchant at a second-hand store who later had sad reason to recall them. From there they made their way south to the little community that was then variously called Goddard, Canyon, or Cañon.

A few years prior, on May 19, 1894, Charles E. Goddard was appointed postmaster for Cañon. Communities often took their names from the person in that position, and with good reason: the shops where locals retrieved their mail became a hub where people connected, supplies were purchased, and a drink might be had. The general store at Goddard's station brought in people from the territory's biggest industries: sheepmen, miners, farmers, and ranchers. Goddard's letterhead proudly and, in elegant print, stated, "C.E. Goddard, Dealer in General Merchandise; Best Brands of Wines and Cigars; Miner's Supplies a Specialty."

Although occasional violence still erupted, what was often referred to as "the Indian problem" was largely quelled by the turn of the century. Cañon - once threatened by Yavapai and Tonto Apache raiders - was a healthy and growing community when Charles and Rosa arrived from California with their two children, Gertrude and her younger brother, Jesse. The younger Goddards helped out with the never-ending work on the ranch, appearing as "farm laborers" on the 1900 census. Theirs was a close family, maintaining regular contact with the extended relations they'd left behind. Certainly Charles and Rosa must have been looking forward to something of a reunion at dinner that February night when Charles' younger brother would once again join them.

The sun had already set when the men sat down to the table in the main house for their meal. It was dark and cool and in the distance a campfire was visible. The two Mexicans interrupted the party to request dinner, but Charles told them they'd have to wait until after the family and guests finished their own meal.

Saying nothing further, the man with the scarred face reached around in his jacket as if to offer payment. Instead, he produced a revolver and immediately began to shoot. Rosa, who'd been preparing dinner in an adjacent room, quickly returned to the dining room when she heard shots.

The concussion of the gunfire snuffed the lamp lighting the house and thrust the room into darkness. The gunmen, unable to see if they had hit anyone, or whom, left the house, leaving the terrified occupants inside and helpless. Hernandez, the sheep shearer still sitting outside on a bench, fled the area upon hearing the gunshots. Charles Goddard, taking a single bullet beneath the heart, was critically wounded. His brother and wife were unable to attend him, crippled by the darkness and the inability to summon medical attention. Rosa ran outside to yell for help, desperately hoping someone would come to their aid from the campsite with the fire in the distance, but as she stepped outdoors she could see the silhouette of one of their attackers hunkered down in wait. She retreated into the building. Charles had managed to move into the next room and onto a couch. There, after an agonizing night shared with the other survivors, he died.

Before finally losing consciousness, Charles told his wife the man who shot him was the scar-faced man. By some accounts, the shooter and his partner remained outside the home for hours, sometimes taunting the people pinned down inside; at times, they manipulated their weapons so the threatening sounds such as hammers being cocked could be heard. Although the Goddard party had weapons and ammunition at their disposal, they were unable to venture outdoors, knowing they would be easily targeted. The murderers were gone by dawn, never able to complete the massacre and robbery they had planned. They'd done damage enough: as sunlight made the devastation visible,

Rosa, Frank Goddard, and Milton Turnbull could see Frank Cocke - whom they thought had escaped in the commotion - slumped over the table, a gunshot wound to the temple. He'd died instantly.

Word of the tragedy was taken south along the stage road by a man named Beasly - or perhaps Garrett, as later accounts stated; his identity has long since passed into obscurity. He notified men at Jim Gibson's ranch and station, where several cowboys who'd been rounding up range horses were encamped. Among them were Jack and Jim Gibson; Wisconsin-born blacksmith Frank B. Moss; William Perry Sears (who went by "Perry"); cattleman Houston C. Ward; and the round-up cook, a black man named Henry Owens. Owens had seen the outlaws that morning as they passed by camp not sixty yards from where he'd slept.

The erstwhile messenger, Beasly or Garrett, also stopped at Frank Alkire's Triangle-Bar ranch and stage stop in New River, just a few miles to the south, to tell the story. Meanwhile, another messenger by the name of Louis Gruell rode toward Prescott to notify the sheriff of the incident. The Maricopa County sheriff at the time, W. W. "Billy" Cook, owned a ranch near New River and was related by marriage to Alkire. By Monday night, he and Sheriff Joseph I. "Joe" Roberts from Yavapai County headed for Gibson's in a buggy, their saddle mounts tied behind, and breakfasted. There, Perry Sears, a married man in his early thirties, joined the lawmen as they made their way back to the crime scene.

Perry Sears made an excellent addition to the posse. In August, 1893, he had killed a murderer and horse thief named Andy Dimond at a ranch northeast of Phoenix. Dimond had drawn down and tried to shoot Sears whilst trying to make an escape, but fortunately the owner of the ranch had unloaded

Dimond's guns the night before. Perry returned fire, thus preventing Dimond from adding an eighth name to his reputed roster of victims.

The three men, following tips from those they encountered along the way, pursued the two outlaws as far south as the Arizona canal. At the southern station on Jim Gibson's ranch, the Mexicans had stocked up on provisions, then retreated into the foothills. At midnight, they resurfaced at a camp where a Mexican sheepherder who worked for a man the newspapers referred to as "Moodyspaugh" (probably the phonetic spelling of the man named "Mudesbaugh," a local rancher) provided them with coffee and a meal. On Tuesday morning, a fellow traveler reported seeing them near Five Points, a star-shaped trading hub in what is now downtown Phoenix. Someone sighted them waiting for a train, taking note they didn't carry the *serape* blanket roll or baggage normally toted by Mexican travelers at the time. The trail having grown cold, the sheriffs gave up the pursuit and by eleven p.m. Tuesday night had safely returned to Prescott.

Lawmen and citizens throughout the territory now actively sought the two fugitives. It soon became evident they were, in all likelihood, the same men who'd murdered two station keepers, Anton Olson and Charles Stewart, in New River in June of 1900. Olson and Stewart had been mercilessly gunned down, one in front of the stage station and one behind. The station had been ransacked and looted. A small band of Mexican men were suspected of the murders and robbery as well as the attempted murder of a prospector, W. H. Rice, but the case quickly went cold. The same men were implicated in several other murders which had occurred in recent years. If, indeed, the same men were responsible, they probably planned on killing everyone at Goddard Station and then taking everything of value.

Within a month of the Goddard killings, various suspects - none of whom were involved - were taken into custody and eventually released. One, Jose Burea, was arrested in Cave Creek. Rosa Goddard was brought into Phoenix to view Burea, but could not identify him; she knew he wasn't the scar-faced man but could not say for sure if he was the man's accomplice. Another, Casimiro Rodelas, was apprehended farther north and held in Prescott. Casimiro Rodelas also had no scar. Hernandez, the sheepherder, was able to immediately say Rodelas was not involved when brought in to look at the man. But by April 1, the two men who would prove to be the culpable parties were found - and it was largely thanks to the scar on the one man's cheek, and a very committed and capable peace officer, that he was identified.

James William "Billy" Blankenship, described by the Prescott *Weekly-Journal Miner* as "one of the best officers in the territory," managed to locate two Mexicans, Elijio Hidalgo and Francisco Rentaria, on the Mexican side of Naco. Rather than contend with extradition issues, he arranged for Hidalgo's supervisor to send him across the border during his shift, whereupon he was arrested. Rentaria was cagier and reluctant to cross the line. With the cooperation of people on both side of the border, Blankenship set up a ruse. Rentaria was told he needed to cash his paycheck at an American bank at a specific time. At the first attempt, Rentaria arrived before the bank was open, nor was the officer assigned to arrest him on site. With the help of a confederate whom Rentaria believed to be a friend, he was again lured across the border and easily taken into custody. Blankenship promptly telegraphed Sheriff Roberts to let him know they had been apprehended. They were initially transported to Phoenix, where Charles Goddard's widow, Rosa, was asked to identify them. She was, however, too distraught and had not seen the suspects long enough in adequate lighting to ensure a positive identification.

Based on the detailed descriptions given by Milton Turnbull and Frank Goddard, though, and corroborated by several statements made by Hidalgo and Rentaria, the peace officers were sure they had the right men. They took them to Prescott and in a proper display of professionalism to avoid contamination of the identification, held them in a room with several other captives when coordinating the eyewitness identifications. They arranged for Francisco Hernandez, the sheepherder, to view them. An apprehensive Hernandez, not knowing why he'd been summoned, immediately and positively identified them as the men with whom he'd had considerable conversation at Goddard's before the killing.

The two suspects were tried in Prescott. In a testament to both the severity and celerity of territorial criminal prosecutions of the early 1900s, within a month of capture they were convicted and sentenced to hang. Although all evidence was circumstantial, it was considered overwhelming and no appeal was sought. The two greeted their fate, as the *Arizona Republican* newspaper put it, insouciantly. At 10:45 in the morning on July 31, 1903, Sheriff Roberts read the death warrant to the two in their cell in Prescott. An interpreter translated the warrant to Spanish. As he finished, Hidalgo laughed and said to him, "I have heard that repeated so often, if that was a song I would sing it to you." After Sheriff Roberts left the cell, the Reverend Father Alfred Quetu of Prescott's Roman Catholic church administered last rites and led the men in prayer.

Hangings were then large, enthusiastically-attended public events. Invitations to executions were printed and sent to influential and prominent citizens. Newspapers sent reporters and illustrators to chronicle the festivities. They were elaborate affairs, employing numerous professionals and tradesmen: from carpenters who built the scaffold to the doctors, peace officers, gravediggers, and clergymen. Certainly executions were an economic boost to the towns where they took place.

At 11:15, the two partners in crime were escorted to the scaffold erected in the city jail yard, led by Father Quetu and accompanied by the hanging party. Newspapers of the day provided great detail in covering the executions: Hidalgo, for example, was positioned on the north trap of the scaffold, while Rentaria stood upon the south. Before being hooded, Hidalgo acknowledged people he knew in the crowd and bid them, and then the crowd at large, "*Adios.*"

Although by the *Arizona Republican* account "the execution was conducted without any unusual incident," by later standards it did not go smoothly. To be as humane as possible, hangings were carefully calculated. The desired result was enough drop or counterweight to ensure the immediate dislocation or fracture of the condemned man's neck - but not so much as to decapitate him (as sometimes happened). Although Hidalgo, prayer book in hand, died instantly after the trap was released at 11:24, Rentaria strangled to death. Apparently Rentaria had been given a folded newspaper which he carried to the scaffold. Witnesses said that as the two were asked if they were prepared, Rentaria moved as if to toss the paper aside. That simple motion caused the rope to move to an incorrect position, preventing the intended dislocation of his neck. Perhaps he died slowly by execution standards - but not nearly as slowly, nor unnecessarily, as Charles Goddard had.

The Yavapai County physician, Dr. Fitzsimmons, declared the men dead at 11:34. He was assisted in his official duties by doctors from Williams, Prescott, and Crown King. Postmortems were done promptly, and by four o'clock, the dead men were buried. From the crime itself to the execution of Elijio Hidalgo and Francisco Rentaria - including apprehension, identification, trial, and sentencing - a mere six months had passed.

Above: General area of the Goddard property as it appears in 2018, looking toward the northwest. (Author photo)

Below: USGS Survey map showing Goddard Station and placement of the store, corrals, barn, and house at the right edge.

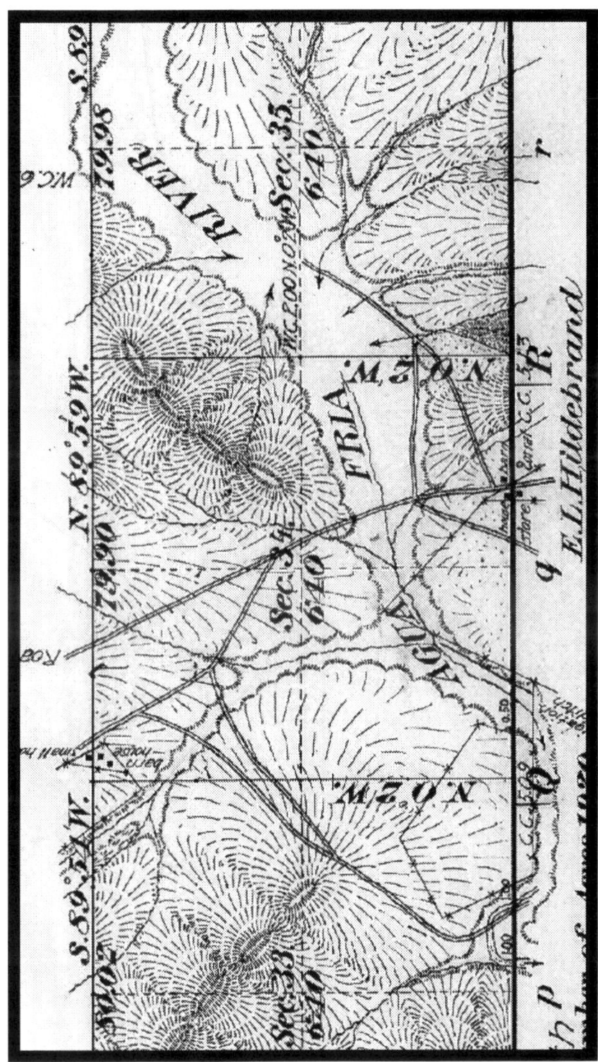

The sickly miner present during the shootings, Milton Turnbull, died later that year. Milton, like his father Luke, was active in mining throughout the state. Despite pursuing medical treatment in Los Angeles in June of 1903, Milton's condition deteriorated. He returned to Denver where most of his family lived and is buried in an unmarked grave in Riverside Cemetery.

The Reverend Father Alfred Quetu, the Roman Catholic priest who ministered to Hidalgo and Rentaria at their execution, went on to become the pastor at California's famous Mission San Juan Capistrano. A French immigrant, he began purchasing ranches in the San Juan area to form a French colony of Roman Catholics. He was fondly remembered in Arizona as a well known priest and a spitfire, quick to scrap with anyone who slandered the church - or his own good name.

Frank Cocke's name was variously spelled "Cox," "Cocke" and "Cockes," in contemporary newspapers.

In the wake of the murders, the two new widows - Rosa Goddard and Frank Cocke's wife - had their husbands' bodies transported to Phoenix for burial. Charles Goddard's funeral cost $192.55, of which $5.00 was allocated for the grave digging. He was buried in Rosedale Cemetery in Phoenix. His will directed that his entire estate - primarily comprised of 160 acres and 400 head of cattle - be left to Rosa. It was valued at under $2,000.

Rosa (whose legal name was "Rose") and her daughter also owned five placer mines and associated water rights in partnership with a woman named Lizzie Moe. The mines were located near Jack Swilling's ranch. In 1913, the trio sold the claims to a man named James Adams for what the newspaper account described as a nominal fee.

Rosa never remarried. Upon her death in January of 1927, her obituary briefly retold the tale of the tragedy, noting it had "shadowed" her life. Her daughter, Gertrude, attended a teacher's college in Maricopa County and moved to Sacramento, California to teach. Gertrude married a man (also named Goddard) with whom she raised a family. Her mother Rosa and brother Jesse also moved to Sacramento in May of 1909, where Jesse completed high school. Rosa returned later to Arizona and lived until her death at the Pioneers' Home in Prescott.

In April, 1909, an affluent Englishman bought Goddard Station - including the 160 acres of land it sat upon - from Rosa for $10. He assured the newspapers he would keep the name. It would not be his only acquisition.

Chapter 4

Hildy and the Polo Ponies

Goddard Station's Second Chapter

The popular imagination has long been captivated by the story of the cultured Englishman bravely facing the rugged western frontier. Lord Darrell Duppa, the classically-educated remittance man, is well known to enthusiasts of Arizona history for his many exploits - among them, giving Phoenix its classically-inspired name. Cañon's own plucky chap E.L. Hildebrand, though, has sadly slipped from popular knowledge and the acclaim he well deserves.

Born in Liverpool, England, on May 18, 1876, Edward L. Hildebrand emigrated to the United States in 1893. Hildebrand was a tall, blue-eyed gentleman of medium build, balding in his maturity. Fond of his newly-adopted home, he became a naturalized citizen in 1896 in Fresno County, California. Somewhere along the course of his travels he met his future wife, a fellow native of England named Esther Mary Steele, and in 1908 he married her in Ohio.

Hildebrand knew and loved horses. An avid polo player, in 1904, prior to moving to Arizona, he lived and played in Los Angeles as an active member of the Los Angeles Polo Club's "Grays" team. One of his winning horses in California was a gray gelding named "Sea Foam." Sea Foam, just the sort of animal Hildebrand sought for polo, was a quick track-tested horse who competed in quarter-mile races.

When racetracks folded after the turn of the 20th century due to bans on bookmaking and races, great quantities of highly-bred Thoroughbred horses were suddenly unemployed. Hildebrand -

affectionately known as "Hildy" to his Arizona friends - saw the opportunity for profit while repurposing the horses he so admired. Hildebrand began shipping unwanted racing stock to England, often selling them to British aristocracy. As he traveled the west, though, he recognized unexpected talent in the agile, tough cowponies he encountered. Rugged, thrifty, and economical, they were already bred for quickness and - most importantly - had an innate drive to chase cows. That instinct, known as being "cowy" to the cowboy, translated handily to chasing a polo ball.

Hildy turned to buying up cowponies directly from ranchers. In 1906, he bought 14 ponies in the Willcox area and had recently sold a $40 cow pony for the equivalent of $2,000 in England. A 1907 account described his endeavor in more detail: he'd pay $60 or more for a pony, ship them to New York for $75, and transport them from there to England for $75. Once in the old country, sporting gentlemen would buy them for $500 to $1,000 each. Hildebrand hired men to oversee the transport while he continued his buying expeditions throughout the southwest. Among the ponies he purchased was a horse named "Coyote" owned by local rancher Billy Cook - the same former Maricopa County Sheriff W. W. "Billy" Cook who initially pursued the Goddard murderers.

Surprisingly, despite clearly being an active and vigorous man, one newspaper account mentions Hildebrand suffered paralysis in 1908 before again coming west. He rebounded well enough to return to his adventurous lifestyle, playing polo, accumulating properties, traveling throughout the country, and managing his horse-export business.

In April, 1909, Hildebrand paid Rosa Goddard $10 for Goddard Station. The *Arizona Republican* said, "The same policy which has made this half way house so popular will be observed by the new owner." Hildebrand rapidly grew in influence, becoming a popular town booster. In 1910 the papers referred to him as "the Goddard merchant" who lobbied for the reopening of the old stage road through Black Canyon to mitigate the time and effort necessary to take supplies to mining sites in the Bradshaws. A later article in Flagstaff's *Coconino Sun* described him as "a genial gentleman whom it is a pleasure to meet." By the 1910 census, the Hildebrand household included Edward and Esther's Chinese cook, a man named Yee Bilkes - one of the many Chinese laborers who contributed to the development and workings of Cañon.

At his ranch in December of that year, Hildebrand lost a good friend who'd come to stay with him. Marshall C. Washburn had met Hildebrand in Arkansas. In the fall of 1909, Washburn - like so many earlier arrivals to Arizona - came to the desert in order to recover from a lung condition. Unfortunately, Washburn didn't recover and died on the ranch in Cañon. Hildebrand personally conveyed his friend's body to Phoenix.

Hildebrand continued acquiring other properties in Cañon and surrounding areas, determined to carve a horse-breeding and polo center out of the desert. By 1912, Hildy had a 320-acre ranch in Cañon (still referred to by some papers as "Goddard" and others as "Gillett" at the time) under development as a polo ground. He kept 250 acres under irrigation that year and operated a farm on the ranch as well as an equestrian center. His horses had the luxury of summering at Flagstaff, where Hildebrand stood a Thoroughbred stallion to local mares at a $25.00 fee.

That stallion deserves mention as well. Named "Dominus Arvi" and valued at $15,000, he was a proven racehorse and the son of the famous imported racehorse Kismet. Kismet, imported to the United States to stand at stud, sold to Australian horse breeders at 21 years old for the whopping sum of $22,000. No doubt owning a Kismet son was a point of particular pride for the horseman's horseman Hildebrand. A 1912 ad in the *Coconino Sun* for Dominus Arvi's stud services described him as "bred by the late Charles Kerr at Bakersfield, California, and by the record is one of the fastest and gamest horses every foaled and developed on the coast. He is today the most highly bred horse in Arizona, and destined to greatly improve its blood stock interests."

It's likely Hildebrand's first son, Robert L., was born in Cañon around 1912. His second son, Geoffrey, came along five years later. By 1913, Hildy had filed homestead paperwork under the 1863 Homestead Act providing three year proof on land near Bumblebee. "Proof" in homesteading terms was the documentation provided to show the homesteader was legally meeting the improvement requirements to purchase the land from the federal government at low prices, and the act of making the improvements was referred to as "proving up."

Not one to stay in one place for long, Hildebrand continued to travel and play polo, and 1915 found him serving as polo manager at a club in Chicago. Hildebrand probably took some of his Arizona polo ponies to Illinois with him; while playing at the club he managed, a fruit jobber named E. L. Hasler, riding a green horse that had just been brought in from the west, was bucked off. Hasler fractured his skull in the accident and was killed. Death touched Hildebrand at every juncture.

Ever the visionary and entrepreneur, by 1918 Hildebrand owned a ranch outside of Las Vegas, New Mexico, called *El Porvenir,* that he successfully operated as a resort. He never moved back to Arizona. Sadly, his wife Esther died just two years later at a youthful 38, leaving him with the two young boys. A grief-stricken Hildebrand returned to England with his sons. In 1923, he died in Worcester. Just in his mid-40s, he'd led a big life. Hildy left his unique mark on Cañon, introducing the quintessential English game of polo to a town where, decades later, polo was still played.

Aftermath and Author's Notes

Traces of the actual Goddard Station are no longer to be found. Using the USGS survey map, I walked the riverside in search of ruins or landmarks that might have been part of the stagecoach stop or ranch. I found nothing tangible, but could easily envision where the old road would traverse the riverbed and where, on the south side of the river and west of where the buildings had stood, the large stock corral would have been. Goddard's, and later Hildebrand's, property extended onto both north and south banks of the Agua Fria.

Hildebrand's property has long since been divided and subdivided. Cañon pays no homage to him; there are no streets bearing his name, no "Hildy Ranch" subdivisions. No portraits - if they even exist - commemorate him at the local museum. Homes and barns have sprung up where sheep once watered and travelers found a hot meal. The Agua Fria has changed the face of the land along its banks, but the site of the brutal Goddard murders - on the south side of the river's bend, north of what is now Squaw Valley Road - still retains a sense of wildness. The leg of the old stage road that once passed through Goddard's property between Phoenix and Prescott was not modernized into the Old Black Canyon Highway, as many of the stage roads were. It had already largely been abandoned by 1909 when Hildebrand purchased the property.

Chapter 5

A Road of Gold

The Uncanny Attraction of the Maggie Mine

Gold mines have an inexplicable pull on the hearts and minds of men and women. They're no easy path to wealth. Mining is dirty, hard, time-consuming labor, but the appeal of extracting something precious from the earth is irresistible to the human spirit. Gold mines have a mystique and mythos all their own, the stuff of dreams and despair and lies and legend.

Mine shafts aren't just a place for discovery of valuable metals. They're a motherlode of potential for hiding and concealing what stuff and secrets men wish to bury. They're a magnet for bodies living and dead. They attract self-sufficient, capable, and often rough men - and women who defy any wilting lily stereotype.

Despite her feminine name, the Maggie Mine is no delicate old lavender-scented lady. Salted with the ashes of some who lived on her grounds, she harbors a history of family feuds, a black-sheep fugitive son, illegal enterprise, suicide, and tangled pioneer pedigrees. Other gold mines in Arizona may have yielded greater wealth - but the Maggie is a treasure trove of scurrilous history. Such is her attraction, people have a strange affinity for returning to the Maggie. They can't let her go.

Perhaps John August Brown, namesake and grandson of the Maggie's original claimant, regretted coming back to Maggie. There, on May 14, 1953, he was approached by a couple of armed men who answered affirmatively when he asked if they were hunters. He reminded them nothing was in season at the time, but they didn't leave empty-handed. They took John

Brown, just shy of his 50th birthday, with them - in handcuffs. Brown had been hiding in the Maggie's shafts during the day, sleeping in his sister's cabin there at night. The two lawmen, sheriff's deputies Lester Jones and Vern LaMore, had been tipped off of Brown's presence and knew he was cagey. They stalked him through the rugged, cactus-covered terrain in darkness and watched for 90 minutes from a nearby hillside until they were tactically prepared to take him into custody.

Brown was a long-time loser. Born June 4, 1903 in what would later be Smokey the Bear's birthplace of Capitan, New Mexico, by 1929 he had already been sentenced to eight to 14 years in prison for embezzlement and fraud - "obtaining money under false pretenses." Somehow, he served only 18 months of that sentence. A 5'7" blue-eyed, brown-haired truck driver at the time, he had but an eighth-grade education and a nascent fondness for young boys. On August 16, 1941, he walked through the doors of San Quentin penitentiary as prisoner #67050, sentenced to four violations of California penal code Section 288. Despite his conviction and a sentence of seven to life on three counts of lewd and lascivious behavior and one count of sexual perversion, John served only seven years before his parole.

In 1945, John registered for the draft, citing his address as simply "Rock Springs." Perhaps his seven-year commitment included time served pre-trial; whatever the circumstance, he was clearly back in the Cañon area for a time. During one of his stays at the Maggie, he distinguished himself by repairing the pothole-challenged road on the property. His father, Archibald B. "Archie" Brown, had been working the mine and left a pile of diggings to be processed. Johnnie, Archie later told a reporter, filled in the potholes with the fruit of his labors. Archie said he ultimately retrieved 57 ounces of gold - then worth $1,000 or so

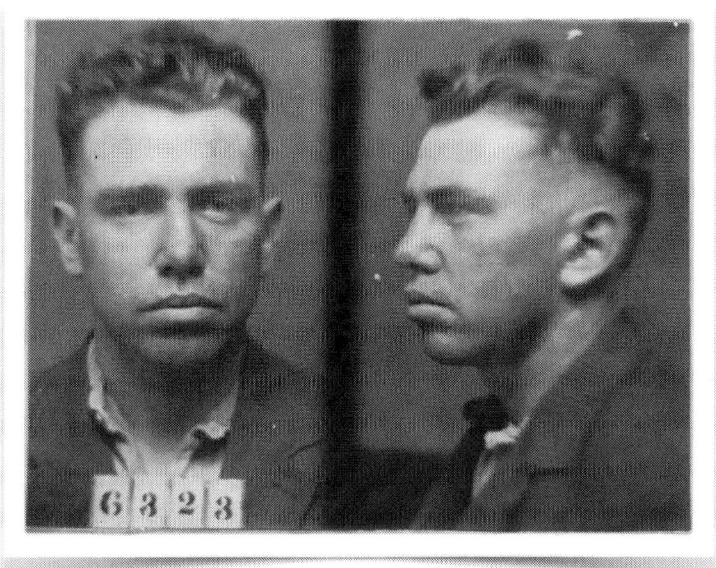

Above: Mug shots of John August Brown taken in New Mexico.

- from his road of gold. John may have had the Midas touch, but in reverse.

John returned to California and his predatory lifestyle. He had family roots in Contra Costa County; his father, Archie Brown had lived in Antioch, as had John's sister, Amelia "Amy." He managed to become involved with a private school in Contra Costa County, where he victimized about a dozen 12 to 16 year old boys. He was charged with "committing and teaching unnatural sex acts" and, knowing he would be looking at possible incarceration for the rest of his life, fled to the Maggie Mine - still owned by his family - to hide.

Unlike his wayward son, Archie Brown was a well-liked man, described in a pair of newspaper columns in 1966 as confident, optimistic, and cheerful despite his vision impairment, advanced age, and a life of many hardships - one of which was certainly his son Johnnie. Born in Pike Run, Michigan on April 12, 1878, he was a long-time railroad man. By 1937, he'd returned to Cañon where his parents, John and Isabella Brown, and his brother James had lived and mined. There, in 1896, his father John had discovered the Maggie lode. Archie did some mining in New Mexico while working for the Santa Fe Railroad, living in Gallup for many years. His mother, Isabella, had been born in New Mexico, and it was in New Mexico Archie met and married a Frenchwoman, Lena Chretien.

Archie and Lena had two sons and three daughters, most of whom were heavily involved with the Maggie at some point. Only his daughter Isabelle remained in New Mexico. Daughters Margaret and Amy lived at the Maggie much of their lives. In 1940, Amy graduated from Glendale (Arizona) High School and, shortly thereafter, moved to Antioch, California, working as a bookkeeper. She married a man named James L. Marglin in 1946, with whom she had a son, Doug. Her sister, Margaret, married to German immigrant Carl Raestle, remained in Arizona.

In 1941, Archie remarried. His new bride, Irene, had been married to a member of the Manifee family, a long-time presence in Black Canyon City and other Arizona mining towns. Tragically, on December 20th, 1943, after just 18 months of marriage and apparently suffering ill health, 62-year-old Irene shot herself above the left ear with a .410 shotgun in the front yard at the Maggie Mine homesite. Archie was away from the home inspecting his mines, but a neighbor heard the gunshot and found Irene's body. He notified nearby highway workers - during those years the Black Canyon Highway was under construction - who then summoned Justice of the Peace J. L.

Above: Archie's footbridge. (Author's photo)

Burleson of Humboldt. The coroner's jury convened by Burleson determined Irene's death to be suicide.

Despite the emotional impact of his wife's gruesome death, Archie stayed on at the Maggie. He had already built the "upper" house on the hill to the west side of the property, where the Black Diamond claim was situated. Around 1951, he gave that house to his eldest daughter, Margaret, and built the lower house - just on the other side of the wash and to the east - on the border of the Black Diamond claim and the Maggie claim. Because the wash separating the properties flowed abundantly with up to eight feet of water during the seasonal rains, Archie built a footbridge across the wash so he could easily walk between the houses. Ruins of the small wooden bridge still remain.

Archie's daughter Margaret died in 1964, survived by her husband of 35 years, Carl Raestle. By now Archie was a widower, had a son in prison, and had lost a daughter to whom he was close. His son-in-law, Carl, with whom he was known to be close friends, briefly moved to Prescott. There, in 1968, Carl married his third wife, a woman of many names: born Ophelia Aethelene Monroe, she went by "Belle." Belle had been married to a man named Thomas Bell, making her Belle Bell - at least until becoming Mrs. Raestle. Carl, like so many others, also returned to the Maggie, bringing Belle back to the Black Diamond homesite that year.

In 1969, at 90 years of age and a veteran of the Spanish American War, Archie Brown passed away at the Fort Whipple Veteran's Hospital in Prescott. His body was sent to Antioch, California, where his daughter Amy then lived. In his will, he left all of his property to Amy. In probate proceedings, Carl Raestle was appointed administrator of the estate. He continued to mine the Black Diamond claim, applying for a patent in 1971. The following July, 1972, Amy Brown Marglin returned to Cañon and once again made the lower house on the east edge of the Maggie property her home. Not even a month later, on August 3, 1972, Carl Raestle died. His widow, Belle, remained at the upper house at the Black Diamond site, across Archie's footbridge from Amy.

While living in California, Amy met a man described in her obituary as "the love of her life" - John VanWyck Whitson, nine years her junior. John, a Navy veteran, had previously been married and raised three children. After several years together, in 1980 John and Amy traveled to Contra Costa County to formally marry - but the Maggie Mine was still home. Amy adored the mine, cherishing the wooden mill house and relics of decades of family and mining history. She proudly kept guest books recording those who visited the site. Amy worked as a waitress at Rock Springs Cafe for years, becoming a much-loved local fixture, while John established himself as an active and popular member of the community.

During the mid-1970s, a group of hard-working community-minded men who patronized the Midway Bar in Cañon evolved into a civic service group they called "The Filthy Five." The original founders were construction workers who wanted to contribute to Cañon by using their skills to build local amenities. The name referred to the dirty hands and fingers gotten by hard work, and the symbol of the club was a hand with each finger signifying a value: *To Work, to Help, to Love, to Give, to Live.* By 1976, the club incorporated as a charitable organization. John Whitson was by then a member, eventually becoming the head fundraiser for the group. The Filthy Five later cleaned up their name and became the High Desert Helpers, responsible for the development of the Filthy Five Park (now called High Desert Park) among other projects. From delivering meals to local shut-ins to hosting a plethora of community events, the organization continues to contribute to the community.

From his battered straw cowboy hat to his close-cropped beard, John Whitson looked every bit Black Canyon. He liked to dance in the grey occasionally on legal issues; local lore has it he was arrested in the front yard at the Maggie Mine as he dressed out an open-range cow that wandered close enough he adopted it as his own. His inclination to avail himself of certain opportunities notwithstanding, John was fondly remembered. Upon his death in 1999, his obituary described him as an "artist."

In the mid-1970s, the Maggie Mine property became embroiled in litigation over property rights. In an oversimplification of a fairly convoluted case, Belle Raestle sued for ownership of Maggie Mine land, claiming a right to the house Archie Brown had left behind as she claimed it sat on land under her mining patent. Had a goat belonging to Amy, the sister of her late husband's deceased wife, Margaret, not eaten Belle's prized roses and pomegranate bush, the suit might never have occurred, but that was the final insult in a perhaps already-strained relationship. In 1975, after the notorious goat incident, Belle sued. Amy prevailed, retaining the lower house, while Belle kept the Black Diamond site and the upper house.

In 1977, Belle remarried. Her third and final husband was Ralph Scandlin, locally known as "Hilljack" on the CB radio he routinely used. Ralph, for a time the editor of the Black Canyon Times, was also active locally. Ralph, too, had been married and widowed with two stepsons from his first wife, Ethel. After Ophelia Aethelene "Belle" Monroe Bell Raestle Scandlin passed away in Sedona in 2007, Ralph Scandlin's stepsons stayed on at the Black Diamond site.

Like her father before her, Amy Whitson endured her own share of hardship from her own son's death to the loss of John Whitson. She, too, was cheerful, outgoing, and optimistic through it all. As she advanced in years and finally retired from Rock Springs Cafe, Amy sought suitable buyers for her beloved Maggie Mine. She found them in bluegrass musicians Jimmy and Shirley Longfellow. The Longfellows bought the Maggie in 2000 after agreeing to keep the Maggie as a mine and a site of historical interest - and to let Amy's ashes be scattered across the land she so loved. Amelia "Amy" Brown Marglin Whitson died in an assisted living center in Peoria on May 31, 2007 at 85 years of age. Her memorial service, during which her ashes were released, was held at the Maggie. Amy, like so many of her family before her, had returned one last time to the Maggie.

Above and below: The old Maggie Mine mill house, 2017. (Author photos)

Amy's ashes aren't alone. Many others had preceded hers, not all of whom were family. On the property today stands an old trailer home, long empty. An old Georgia-born miner, known as "Uncle Miltie," lived and died in the trailer at the Maggie. Miltie - Milton Edgar - had moved to Arizona from Escondido, California, where he, his wife Muriel, and his mother Nellie had been members of an infamous theosophical organization of the 1930s known as the "I Am," movement. Interestingly, the "I Am" movement was founded by a fellow mining man, mining engineer named Guy W. Ballard. After Ballard's death in 1939, some of the leaders of "I Am" were charged with mail fraud amidst allegations they operated a "sham" religion. Miltie (who was not known to be involved in any impropriety involving the movement) began mining in Arizona around that time with his partner, Charles Sindelar of Los Angeles. In 1940 they purchased the Last Chance Mine outside of Florence from Ace and Mary Tomerlin of the Black Canyon area, as well as purchasing the Zona claim from Ace and one of his partners, J. W. Allison. Miltie made other area claims as well. Upon Uncle Miltie's death at 83 years old on August 27, 1996, his ashes, too, were spread at the Maggie.

Dozens of mining claims registered to the Browns are marked by names relevant to the family and its history: the Isabella, Jim, Jolly John, Maggie, Archibald, Bella, Gallup, Black Cañon. Archie's brother, James, patented many, as did his son Robert. Even Lena, Archie's first wife, carried a patent on a claim, as did ill-fated Irene, Archie's second wife. The old mining patents bear nostalgic tribute to the now-vanished Browns of Maggie Mine, and the Maggie is honored by giving her name to Maggie Mine Road.

Above: Uncle Miltie's trailer at the Maggie Mine. (Author photo)

The Longfellows shared a rumor with me that a body had been disposed of in the vertical mine shaft. If true, it was likely the body of Air Force Sgt. Lawrence Broughall. In a brutal act of betrayal, in 1969 Broughall's body was unceremoniously dumped after his go-go girl ex-girlfriend and her biker buddies conspired to murder him. Black Canyon, people say, has a reputation as a popular place to dump bodies.

Aftermath and Author's Notes

The structures at the Maggie Mine are lovingly tended. The mill house, complete with implements used to process the ore, is likely the best such structure remaining in the Cañon area. The mine shafts and tunnels themselves have been sealed to prevent entry; rumor has it one of the entries was destroyed to conceal certain illicit activity that occurred within. Such activity may have been related to the marijuana grow operation abandoned in a ravine ridge adjacent to the property. While doing some work

Above: Remnants of the marijuana grow site east of the Maggie Mine. (Author photo)

on the water supply at the property, the Maggie's owners, the Longfellows, followed some irrigation lines across the rugged terrain to find remnants of the former pot farm: terracing, pots, shelter, and a water source, cleverly hidden by the brush and topography.

Above: Ruins at the Maggie Mine. (Author photo)

For this chapter I relied largely on newspaper archives, court documents, mining claim records, and numerous official records such as correctional records, vital records, and land records. Site visits included the Maggie Mine property and vicinity. Many of the people I interviewed knew and loved Amy Whitson and shared fond memories of Amy and John Whitson, Uncle Miltie (Edgar Milton), and others associated with the Maggie. Shirley and Jimmy Longfellow kindly gave me a tour of the Maggie Mine and enthusiastically shared their love and knowledge of its history.

Chapter 6

And Bones Washed Up

The Healing Clay of Mud Springs

At about 1:12 p.m. on May 6, 1971, laborers working the cotton crops southwest of the farming community of Coolidge looked to the sky. Above, a twin-engine DeHavilland Dove struggled audibly; witnesses said they heard the plane's engines stop, then restart. Stunned, the workers watched as it plummeted to earth in a near nose-dive. The Phoenix-bound Apache Airlines plane, not even twenty minutes past its uneventful departure in Tucson, was estimated to have been flying at about 250 knots - about 287 miles per hour - when it faltered. It destroyed the concrete culvert it struck, releasing irrigation water onto neighboring fields, and erupted in flame.

All twelve people aboard Flight 33 were killed. It was a gruesome scene. Wreckage and carnage were strewn over 100 square yards across the farmland. The condition of the casualties was consistent with such violent impact. Long-time Phoenix-area FAA investigator Myles Ruggenberg said he'd "never seen anything like it." It was the first commercial airliner crash in the country since November, 1969.

The president of Apache Airlines, George Dembow Jr., just five days shy of his 38th birthday, responded to the horrific scene. He aptly described it as "utter devastation." Three of the pilots from his small fleet of aircraft were on board - two as crew, and one as a passenger - as well as another of the airline's employees and the latter victim's fiancee. The blow to Mr. Dembow wasn't just the intensely personal trauma of visiting a particularly grisly multiple-casualty scene involving friends and employees - the event ultimately grounded the airline. Dembow didn't know, as he studied the debris, he was seeing the wreckage of five years of his personal and financial investment scattered across that field.

Apache Airlines had struggled since its 1957 inception. Its founder, M. L. "Babe" Clements, sold it to a man better known for his national chain of Arizona-headquartered service stations. Monroe Blakely, despite his prowess at managing his gas station line, saw his airline business go into bankruptcy by 1965. That led to purchase for $245,000 by a company incorporated as Caravan Airlines. By the following year, Apache sold again - for the third time in six months - to a New York businessman, Sigmund Sommer, for half a million dollars. Sommer, a frequent winter visitor to Arizona, was inexperienced in the aviation business. He may have already had a plan in mind when the struggling airline came across his radar. For years he'd tried to convince a fellow New Yorker to come work for him. That friend was then thriving as the vice president of the largest electrical contracting company, Fishback & Moore. The offer Sommer made to George Dembow Jr. was too appealing to Dembow's particular personality traits to pass up.

An Air Force veteran who specialized in formation flying, Dembow had a jet pilot's confidence, love of adventure, and passion for taking on a new challenge. "That's why no one was ever comfortable driving with him," recalled his wife, Ethelanne, "because he drove the way he flew. It was that character trait that made him able to pursue what a lot of others would think oh boy, that's too out of reach." Sommer called Dembow and said, "George, I want to buy a little airline out here - and I don't want any part of it - will you come buy part of it at a very advantageous price. Will you come out and run it for me?" He offered Dembow a half-interest in the venture for

$50,000 and Dembow's perfectly-suited managerial skills. It was an irresistible offer.

Ethelanne remembered the weekend Dembow flew to Phoenix to meet with Sommer. "I knew when he came back, the way he talked about it - the struggling airline that was losing money - I knew if he didn't accept the challenge, he would always wonder what kind of man was he. He had no doubt, and he did! He made it work! He went from purchasing part of a losing proposition to - in just two months - starting to make money." Dembow, with characteristic energy and vision, wasted no time in improving and modernizing the airline. Propellor planes were replaced with turbo-prop jet craft. Despite the obstacles thrown before the airline by aviation officials, who protected government-subsidized carriers, Dembow sought to expand Apache's routes.

By the time Apache Flight 33 hurtled to earth, the airline's prospects were solid. Profits, for an unsubsidized small fleet, were perennially tight, but FAA supervisors described the airline as having an "excellent safety record," and Arizonans loved having air service to small communities throughout the region. Residents enthusiastically greeted service to then-small towns such as Kingman, Lake Havasu, Sierra Vista, and Douglas. For the time-pressed traveler, such as Thomas Segundo, the airline offered opportunities to make it to engagements that were otherwise impossible. Segundo, chairman of the Papago Tribal Council, perished in the crash.

Never a friend to the airline, the Federal Aviation Authority was instrumental to Apache's demise. The planes had been modified with a part specified by the FAA, Ethelanne Dembow said. And after the crash, the FAA, based on the fact the few remaining planes in the fleet had the same modification, grounded the airline. Hemorrhaging money by the day, unable to service its flights, and now in bankruptcy proceedings again without a willing buyer, the fourteen-year-old airline shut down.

A hundred miles from the site of the downed Dove, the aging children of homesteader Anna K. Crawford pondered what to do with their 80-acre homestead in Cañon. They'd tried to sell the property over the years but it had doggedly remained in family hands. It wasn't the ordinary rangeland or cropland found in the area. It boasted a unique and rare feature: more than a dozen mud springs along a fault line in the earth. Water percolated up through mineral-dense mud and, although the water wasn't palatable, the mud was long-renowned for its healing properties.

In 1948, the Crawford family posted an ad in the Arizona Republic describing the property as "Mud Springs: A potential health resort only a few miles from Phoenix in a very picturesque spot just off the new Black Canyon Highway. There are 14 mud springs concentrated in a 2 acre area of the 80 acres in the entire place, a 3-bedroom modern home, several 2-apt. cabins and a bath house. The owners have been there many years and can relate many beneficial results in arthritis, rheumatism and especially skin cases. Now the owners are along in years and want to retire. Development could make this one of the finest health resorts in Arizona."

A Tom Tarbox column a year later indicated the family was still in ownership of the land and a lot of mud at Mud Springs. Tarbox was a local celebrity of sorts: a popular writer for the *Arizona Republic* who wrote in a distinctly chatty, colloquial style, often covering doings in the more remote corners of the valley. His March 5, 1949 column informed us "Mrs. Russell Cross of 2317 North Evergreen Street dropped in to tell us that her brother, Sid Crawford, is living on 40 acres out Black Canyon Highway way, about 52 miles from Phoenix, and Sid's pretty excited about the mud out thataway. There are no less than 14 cold water springs on the place, which are a lot of springs for Arizona, and they've named the place Mud Springs. Miz Cross says the mud is good for a sight of ailments including arthritis, rheumatiz, and sechlike, and anybody so afflicted is welcome to come out and cart away a bucketful or two and no questions asked. 'Ed Meek made some of it into a beauty pack,' said Miz Cross. 'Ed's been trying it out on himself and he's getting so handsome that when he shaves himself, he thinks the fellow in the mirror looking back at him is Clark Gable.'"

The Mrs. Russell Cross he wrote of - Margaret M. Cross - had been raised on the property. Born to Anna Maria Kunselman Crawford and William Walter Crawford in 1905, she and her family moved to the homestead from New Kensington, Pennsylvania in 1916. The family matriarch, Anna, was a registered nurse who specialized in the care of "lungers" - the name given to the hordes of people who came to Arizona territory for the treatment of consumption, properly known as tuberculosis. In the Mud Springs property, Anna recognized the potential of healing those gravely ill individuals. Throughout the southwest, "lungers" flocked to hot springs and sanatoriums. Doctors at the time believed the clear, dry desert air and the breathing room of the then-sparsely populated region to be therapeutic. Sanatoriums had contributed significantly to the state's population and economy, and Anna had experience managing such sanatoriums.

The mud at Mud Springs had a longtime reputation. Locals said the native Yavapai, when leaving their seasonal home in the valley for the cooler mountains to the north every summer, took with them the mud as a beauty remedy and a treatment for barb wire injuries to their horses' legs. Not long after the turn of the century, a group of valley men had formed a company around the property and its famed mud. Comprised of a miner, J. D. Marlar, a mineralogist and miner named H. H. Udell, a lumberman named T. W. Chamberlain, and a pioneer named A. H. Wormell, the partners marketed the mud as a cure for conjunctivitis and other disorders. A June, 1903 blurb in the *Arizona Republican* boasted of the mud's ability to cure the eye disorder. "It has generally been found difficult to do anything for the reduction of the inflammation, so that it is commonly allowed to reduce itself but a new remedy for it has been accidentally discovered in the mud from the mud springs north of Phoenix which is gradually coming to be looked upon more and more as a cure-all."

By 1906 the property, then known as "Mineral Springs" in the community known at the time as "Goddard" was sold for around $16,000, including a large part of payment in stock shares of the future company, to a partnership headed by Los Angeles doctor V. C. Miller. Miller saw in the springs an opportunity to exploit the influx of tubercular patients and other "health tourists" by building a number of sanatorium buildings, creating a health resort. In October, one of Dr. Miller's partners, George F. Whitmore, traveled to Mud Springs to inspect the property and plan for development. The company the men formed was called "The Arizona Wonderine Company."

By 1908 the venture had declined and was in litigation. The September 3, 1908 newspaper carried the headling "Injunction Issues to Stop Stock Sale: The Arizona Wonderine Company is Tied Up in Litigation." The original sellers - all of whom lived in Arizona but for partner George Rogers, of Los Angeles - had been assessed a penny per share on the stock they'd been offered in the company in partial payment for the property.

As a result of the lawsuit, the grandiose sanatorium and spa the men had envisioned, which had proposed to offer "all the conveniences the sick will require," never did spring from the unique clay of the land. It was Anna K. Crawford who would carry on the mens' dream. Under provisions of the 1863 Homestead Act, Anna purchased and "proved up" the land, receiving the patent on August 21, 1931. The Crawford family built several amenities, including a stone bathhouse and five different mud pools for visitors to soak in. The grayish mud bubbled to the surface from a fault in the earth. Animals - cattle and wildlife - had perished in the viscous clay and sometimes, the owners noted, bones washed up. For that reason, the land had not been viable as rangeland. Cattle would be entrapped, drawn by the scent of water and lethally drawn into the mud.

The Crawfords hosted sundry visitors at the humble resort situated about a mile and a quarter east of the old Goddard Station. One guest of note, Dr. Charles Willard Hayes, stayed at Mud Springs with his wife while doing his surveys in Arizona. Head of the United States Geological Study, Dr. Hayes was considered the highest ranking scientist in the nation at the time. The Crawfords also began selling packs of mud from the springs for those who wished to employ its curative properties in their own homes.

For all the family's dreams and efforts, the property never became the luxurious health resort they'd intended. The work was rudimentary, though certainly adequate for its time and purpose. Guest ranches of the time were rustic and accommodations were often crude. Travelers didn't visit for the posh ambience of today's Scottsdale; they visited for western adventure - and for their health. It wasn't uncommon for the day's most elegant stars to spend time at such guest ranches; nearby Rock Springs was honored by a visit from Jean Harlow and, just down the road a few miles in New River, Wrangler's

Roost hosted a member of the Rockefeller clan, among other luminaries.

Whether due to healing mud or not, Anna Crawford and the five children raised on the homestead - Sarah, Margaret, Lavern, Sidney, and Walter - had good long lives. When 88-year-old Anna passed away at her home in Phoenix on August 24, 1963, Mud Springs was still in the family. By 1972, Anna's son Walter worked at Sky Harbor Airport in Phoenix. There, he had forged a friendship with a tall, charismatic businessman who co-owned and operated a small fleet of commuter airlines out of the old, grand Terminal One. When the airlines foundered after the crash of Flight 33, Tom suggested to the airline's president that he buy the family homestead.

George Dembow Jr. reacted with bemused curiosity and a "Why?" Crawford told him the story of the Mud Springs, suggesting Dembow package and sell the mud as a beauty aid. Intrigued, Dembow accompanied Crawford to the site and obtained samples of the mighty mud. Visionary but prudent, Dembow shipped off samples of the mud to dermatologists and laboratories and commissioned a geological assessment. Dembow wasted no time in his new endeavor: by May 25, 1972, but a year and 19 days after the fateful crash, he had in his hands a full geological report describing the mineral composition and properties of the clay comprising the Mud Springs mud.

Running in a northerly line on the western edge of the Crawford property on the east side of Mud Springs Road, the geologist found eight mud springs. Buried within Scientese such as, "Diffracto-grams were run on a General Electric XRD-6 diffractometer at 1 degree / min. gonimometer speed from 3 degrees to 60 degrees two theta," is the estimate that 840 tons of mud were available in those eight mud springs, and that they contained 14 minerals - notably montmorillonite, Kaolinite, and plagioclase minerals - and an absence of harmful materials or bacteria.

Montmorillonite, also known as "Fuller's earth," may not sound familiar to the non-geologically inclined. It's a primary ingredient of the popular, multi-purpose bentonite clay used industrially, cosmetically, and as a home remedy. George Dembow, recognizing the national trend toward ecology-themed products and a fondness for nostalgia, was interested in the cosmetic angle. He purchased Mud Springs for $1,000 an acre and enlisted his family in his bold new enterprise, Arizona Natural Resources. Ethelanne devoted herself to the business from their home while the Dembows' sons, George III and Paul, were drafted to dig and process the mud. They branded the mud packs "Down to Earth" and set out to build a business quite literally from the ground up.

Right: George Dembow Jr. digging the mud at Mud Springs, 1973.

George Dembow III recalled the mud-digging expeditions well. They dug from the most easily accessible spring. Roads in the area weren't well maintained in the 1970s and during the rains, muddy roads made the mud gathering challenging. The mud springs had a distinctive feel. "I remember very clearly, when you'd stand on it, it felt like a trampoline. The surface looked dry. It looked different because the color of the clay was different than sand or dirt. We'd dig down and get the fresh clay, rather than the crust, because things would get trapped in it. I'd heard animals would get trapped in it. I never saw any bones myself but I'd heard of them. The water itself was not palatable; it was very salty." The boys would shovel the clay into five-gallon buckets, haul them home in the back of a pick-up, and dry them. They'd screen the mud, bake it at 540 degrees to kill any bacteria, pulverize it, and reconstitute it with distilled water. They'd then add a preservative to protect against contamination the clay would be exposed to after being opened and finally, they'd package it in a jar.

George Dembow Jr. took a hands-on approach to marketing. Shirtless, shovel in hand, his photograph appeared in a memorable ad placed in four leading women's magazines of the time, such as *Cosmopolitan*. He traveled personally across the country, from Honolulu to Baltimore, touting his product at department stores such as I. Magnin and Robinson's. Local newspapers enthusiastically carried stories about Dembow's magic mud, and often Dembow was the focus more than the product. "He was charming and outgoing," Ethelanne said, and "perfectly suited" to the sales and public contact. Dembow made appearances on "What's Your Line," and other shows. Who would guess a line of work selling … mud?

With a visionary leader and his talented team at work, the beauty packs sold. "George and I were both brought up in New

York … and George used publicity companies in NY. He used top people and it really worked," Ethelanne Dembow said. Their son, George, said, "Dad's creed from the beginning was he wanted to know that we made absolutely the best product that was out there."

The venture soon outgrew the Dembow home. "We had the office in our den at home, and then in a couple of rooms at 33rd ave and Indian School," Ethelanne said. "My husband realized we had to expand but not until we had sold the mud so well that we were saying, 'We'll never have to do anything again! Look at us!'" Eventually, the sales slowed. "And then a customer wanted to return it and said it wasn't selling very well, and then we had to give their money back, and then there was more of a flood of customers who said it wasn't selling very well, and we realized we'd have to do something." At that point, in the mid- to late 1970s, George met with a couple in California who manufactured a line of cosmetics. "They checked one another out, and they were thrilled he wanted to buy their business and their expertise," Ethelanne said. George told customers who wanted to return unsold mud he was unable to return their money - but he could give them cosmetic products with their own business name on it.

Private labeling was a great success. As the concept caught on, department stores from J. C. Penney to Neiman Marcus wanted their own house labels on high-quality cosmetics. Ultimately, Arizona Natural Resources outgrew its Down to Earth mud line. Their shift to other products, combined with industrial use of montmorillonite mud in fracking and the subsequent large-scale mud mining necessary to produce it, rendered the Dembow's mud-digging irrelevant. "Through that humble start it has now been 45 years," George Dembow III said. "It has provided well. We have 100 people we're supporting here." In 1992, Arizona Natural Resources moved into its newly-constructed building in north Phoenix. Ethelanne managed the interior design of the attractive office space, honoring the company's beginnings with details such as the printer's plates for George's early ads.

In 2015, the confident Air Force pilot, businessman, and entrepreneur George Dembow Jr. passed away at age 81. He left behind an innovative business that remains in the Dembow family. His son George Dembow III took the reins as president, and *his* son Josh Dembow works as company compliance officer. In a nod to the company's earthy roots, George Dembow III plans to reintroduce the Down to Earth product line, mud and all.

Right: A 1973 ad in a Hawaii newspaper for Down-to-Earth mud mined from Mud Springs. George Dembow Jr. was personally on hand to meet customers at the J. C. Penney's store in Honolulu.

Aftermath and Author's Notes

The old Mud Springs homestead is now in private hands. The low, hand-set rock wall surrounding the property is reminiscent of the rustic but picturesque guest ranches of the early-to-mid 1900s. The property off of Old Mud Springs Road, advertised for sale in 1948 as an 80 acre health resort, has been subdivided. One portion which had a productive mud spring is now reduced to a parcel just over an acre in size.

The last of Anna Crawford's Mud Springs-reared children have long since passed on. Anna left behind many grandchildren and great-grandchildren.

Healing clay, such as "Bentonite green clay," is still widely used, not just for cosmetic uses, but for veterinary purposes - just as the Yavapai used the Mud Springs mud. I keep it on hand for my own horses' leg injuries and have used it many times on my own wounds.

One of the many great pleasures of this book was spending time meeting with descendants of those whom I wrote about. For this chapter, I visited the Dembow family - Ethelanne Dembow, George Dembow III, and his son Josh - at their business, Arizona Natural Resources. They graciously shared stories and information. I also did extensive research using newspaper archives, official records, homestead documents, land histories, etc.

I visited the Mud Springs area many times to eyeball the properties that were once part of the original Crawford homestead.

The illustration on the first page of this chapter is my original linocut of a DeHavilland Dove DH-104.

Chapter 7

Leo and the Wonder Bus

A Cañon Homesteader Pioneers an Early RV

Leo Riley Leaden loved to drive fast and drive long. His reputation for car racing competition was such that when he challenged Harry Harrington to a Hudson race in New Mexico in June, 1920, Harry's acceptance made the local papers. In the fall of that year, Leaden's car overturned during a race at the county fair in Gallup. Leaden escaped life threatening injury, but suffered a broken arm. If it slowed him down in his driving, it didn't slow him down in his other endeavors. Driving continued to be a large part of his life, albeit at a tourist-friendly pace: he became nationally respected for his driving tours of the southwest, particularly on the Navajo and Hopi lands.

Born September 6, 1891 in Alma, Kansas, Leaden was brought to the southwest at three months old. His parents, Thomas and Catharine, settled in Gallup, New Mexico. Like many westerners who lived lives that require no embellishment to be fascinating, Leo liked to tell stories now and then; for reasons entirely his own, he told a reporter that until his enlistment in the Navy during World War I, his last name was "Leyden," and Leo did, in fact, use that name on occasion. However, newspaper accounts of his father's activities in 1895, long before Archduke Franz Ferdinand's demise, clearly cite Thomas Leaden - not Leyden - in Gallup news.

Despite being busy both making and raising the children who came after Leo - Frank, Anna, Gertrude, Celia, Willie, and Thomas - Leo's industrious father often made the papers. An elected official in Gallup, Thomas was an oil man and property owner who served on the board of directors of the Gallup Oil

Association. He passed down his love of politics to Leo, who campaigned for various public offices throughout his lifetime with varying degrees of success. Leo's destiny, despite his ability to tell an occasional tall tale, wasn't as a professional politician. Six-foot tall, black-haired and hazel-eyed and a trim 165 pounds, he looked every bit the western adventurer he was: a hands-on man who craved action. In 1916, before America entered the Great War, a group of Gallup men proposed a troop of Rough Riders. Leo was among the 20 who enrolled. On May 4, 1917, Leo - at the time working as a miner - enlisted in the Navy at the El Paso enlistment station. He served for 27 months as a Machinist's Mate during the war. It was, he later recounted, the only time he spent living outside the southwest. He was a desert lifer, though, and returned to Gallup after the war.

By 1922, Leo operated guided tours throughout Arizona and New Mexico, concentrating on Navajo and Hopi lands. As an advocate of exploring the then-wide open west, he published roadmaps and travel guides of the roads between Taos and Needles, called "Leaden's Old Trails Road Guide," which sold by the thousands to garages and chambers of commerce who then distributed them as complimentary copies. The maps indicated points of interest and available services along the way, meticulously noted by Leo during his many road trips.

Leo gained a reputation as one of the nation's top experts in the culture of the southwest's natives and reputedly spoke Navajo. It's likely he learned the language growing up in Gallup; he'd said he'd worked as an Indian trader, and consistent with that, in 1913 he cited his occupation as "General Merchandise" in the Gallup directory. His familiarity with the Indians was useful in his tours. In 1924, he advertised a three-day "Snake Dance Special" tour running out of Gallup via the Painted Desert and the Petrified Forest (which he called the "Black Petrified Forest" in his ads). The entire tour cost only $50 per person. That year, he sought the Democratic nomination for sheriff against the incumbent in Gallup, Sheriff Lou Myers, but lost his bid for candidacy. His tour business thrived, though. He rubbed noses with interesting visitors, giving tours to English author D. H. Lawrence (who owned a ranch near Taos for a few years) and the Crown Prince of Sweden. During the mid-20s popular American author (and critic of American culture) Sinclair Lewis toured with Leaden as he worked on his controversial novel *Elmer Gantry.*

Leaden suffered a health condition that precipitated his move to Arizona in 1927. It's likely he was already fighting the tuberculosis that would ultimately kill him. "Lungers" - the slang term for tuberculosis sufferers - had long been coming to Arizona for the dry, clean air that was considered life-extending, if not life saving. Despite his ill health, in typical Leaden fashion he quickly established himself as a presence in the community. On May 8, he was initiated at the historic St. Mary's Church - along with 37 other men - into the Knights of Columbus. St. Mary's (now known as St. Mary's Basilica) had been founded in 1881 and had been long run by Franciscan friars. Leo also joined the American Legion and the Disabled American Veterans of the World War.

Leaden began working for the prominent businessmen, the McArthur brothers, as a guide and driver for their tour and hospitality business. Arizona's tourism business blossomed in the 1920s, proving to be economically important, and the visionary McArthur brothers invested heavily in the industry. They partnered in the founding and construction of the Biltmore resort and, despite the lion's share of fame assumed by Frank Lloyd Wright, Albert Chase McArthur designed and superintended the construction of the well-known facility.

Having worked with Lloyd Wright in the past, McArthur contacted him to inquire about employing the textile block construction technique Lloyd Wright had extensively used. Lloyd Wright was gracious enough to sell the rights to the patented technique to the McArthur brothers, even though he didn't own the patent, causing a future legal battle for the Biltmore. Typical of his well-known arrogance, Lloyd Wright claimed architectural credit for the Biltmore despite disparaging it to Albert McArthur when he first saw the completed structure.

Above: The Biltmore Wonderbus. Photo: Arizona Biltmore collection.

The McArthurs catered to their guests' interest in the western landscape and Indian culture with a tour bus - basically converting a Dodge truck into what some referred to as a "hotel on wheels" - called the "Four Person Wonder Bus." Working out of the McArthurs' headquarters at 306 E. Van Buren in Phoenix, Leo Leaden drove this crude forerunner to the RV. In 1929, the *Arizona Republican* praised him as one of the "four or five best guides in the United States." Unsurprisingly, the capable Leo Leaden rose to manager of the tour branch of the McArthurs' business.

Like many of Black Canyon's homesteaders, Leaden lived in Phoenix for work. His residence at 22 E. Virginia was then in a respectable uptown neighborhood, but as an outdoorsman and desert enthusiast it's no wonder Leaden was drawn to the rugged foothills of Black Canyon. He chose a 120-acre parcel extending roughly to what is now Perry Road to the north, bordered at about the current Mountain View on the south, at about Gayla on the west, and east of Siesta Trail on the east. Leaden received his patent on May 27, 1937. Homesteads took at least five years to "prove up," indicating Leaden had begun his work on the property during the first years of the 1930s or before; it's possible Leaden applied for the property during the late 1920s. Because of the harshness of the desert climate, Arizona homesteaders often took longer to establish the residence portion of homesteading requirements than those in environments more amenable to year-round agriculture.

Leaden's homesteading neighbors during the 1930s included Anna Crawford of Mud Springs and Joe Schell. The latter was one of the area's influential and active citizens - as well as being the first person in Cañon to have a motorized car. Although Leo Leaden's relatives no longer reside in Black Canyon City, the Schell family is one of the many homesteading families who remain in (or affiliated with) the town. As for Crawford, having a registered nurse who managed tuberculosis sanatoriums next door would have been fortuitous for Leo.

In 1941, 51-year-old Navy veteran Leo registered for the WWII draft. His address remained on 22 E. Virginia in Phoenix. He was unemployed at the time and had no telephone. He provided A. E. Sisson, Santa Fe ticket officer, as the name on his draft card of a person who would always know how to contact him. As an effect of his tuberculosis, Leo was already wasting away. His weight had dropped to a gaunt 153 pounds - and he suffered from a broken fourth finger on his left hand at the time of registration.

Still, in 1942, he was a candidate for U.S. Representative, according to the *Tucson Daily Citizen*. Articles announcing his candidacy stated he'd been a hard-rock and coal miner and had worked as a locomotive fireman. Leaden also told the paper he'd moved to Phoenix in 1924 (although he'd told the New Mexico reporter he moved to Phoenix in 1927). A registered Democrat, his pro-America, pro-right-to-work, pro-veteran, and anti-bureaucracy political stance was more aligned with contemporary Republican positions. Leaden, with his long-time commitment to the native people of the nation, sought to give them more input into their affairs with minimal federal interference. He also expressed concern about Arizona's water future, supporting construction of a dam north of Lee's Ferry on the Colorado. Leaden hoped to see more efficient use of military contractors, specifically shipbuilders. In a statement giving a sense of his candor and directness, Leaden told the *Arizona Republic* in February of 1942 he wanted to see a "'shaking down' of the 'build-and-sink' shipbuilding system so as to guarantee the 'taxpayers and the crews who man our ships something better than floating Dunkirks in time of war.'" Not without merit, he also suggested immediately drafting "all foreign refugees who are able-bodied and of military age."

With only 452 votes in the primary, Leo Leaden was unsuccessful in his desire to serve in Congress. Sadly, his health failed him and later that year, at 4:20 p.m. on Christmas Day, he died at the Veteran's Administration Hospital in Tucson at only 51 years of age. His death certificate cited pulmonary hemorrhage due to tuberculosis as cause of death, noting he also had cardiac disease. He'd spent the last 24 days of his life in the hospital, a tragic ending for an active, adventurous westerner.

Aftermath and Author's Notes

Leo Riley Leaden was buried in Hillcrest Cemetery, Gallup, near his baby sister, Celia. Just 20 years old, Celia had also died in December, 22 years before Leo's death.

I was unable to confirm with certainty any marriages or offspring for Leaden.

Below: Leo Leaden's Black Canyon City homestead consisted of the two blocks shown in the most deeply shaded portion to the right side of the center square.

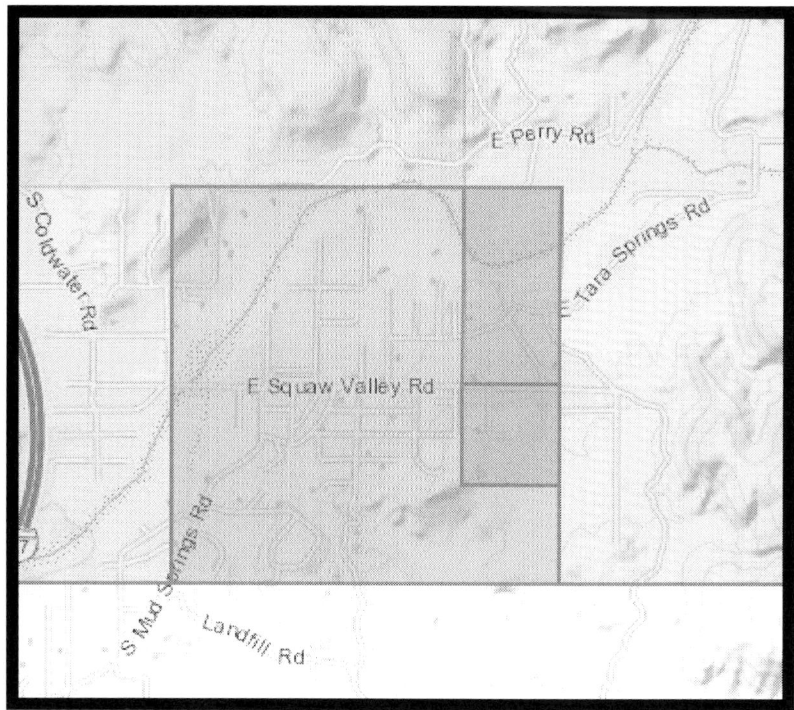

I first saw Leo Leaden's name as nothing more than the name of the owner on a homestead record, and, as is my habit, I began researching the man behind the name looking for an interesting story. To my surprise, I found the story of a fascinating man of the type who contributed tremendously to the Arizona of the early 20th century. I used newspaper accounts from Arizona and New Mexico; official documents and public records ranging from homestead patents to census records and draft registrations; and online histories.

The illustration at the beginning of this chapter is my original linocut block print portrait of Leo Leaden.

Chapter 8

And a Stranger Was Milking Our Cow

The Desert Fox Passes Through

Highway Patrolman Paul Marston wanted to be the one to capture Danny Lee Eckard. The fugitive known as "the Desert Fox" hadn't hurt anybody during his well-publicized prison escapes and flights from justice. He told his fellow officer, Ronald Lee Mayes, that he figured if he was on the scene he could keep Eckard from being injured or killed by quick-triggered officers. On June 9, 1969, Mayes was on his first day's patrol in the district Marston worked. Mayes had just transferred from Globe four days before, and Marston was introducing him to the area and people. Marston was on his last scheduled day in the district, as his transfer to Phoenix was to take effect the next day.

Officers throughout the state had been searching extensively for Eckard. A four-year veteran of the Marine Corps and an expert in desert survival, Eckard had gained the undeserved sympathy of many members of the public. Although there was nothing heroic about him, his ability to elude officers, his desert survival skills, and his habit of taking hostages, treating them politely, and later releasing them had won over the popular imagination. The media dubbed Eckard "the Desert Fox," in recognition of his abilities at escape and elusion. Local radio DJs recklessly fed the notion Eckard was, if not a sort of Robin Hood, at least an underdog to whom people could relate.

When Marston heard the dispatcher broadcast that Eckard was in the area, fleeing in a stolen truck from yet another hostage-taking, he immediately sped toward the ongoing pursuit.

Several officers from multiple agencies were already on Eckard's tail. The high-speed pursuit, sometimes exceeding 120 miles per hour, ended at Four Winds Farm, a horse ranch east of Chino Valley in Perkinsville. Within minutes, three of those officers were wounded - one mortally - and the Desert Fox would be lying in the dirt in a pool of his own blood.

Despite Officer Marston's concern for Eckard, and the public's romanticization of his exploits, Eckard was a violent and dangerous man. After his military service (none of which was in combat), he and his truck-driver father, Rupert, resided at 9512 N. 13th Street in the Sunnyslope neighborhood of Phoenix. Eckard, a wiry 5'8" 160-pounder, spent a lot of time in the desert. A truck driver for a furniture store, he enjoyed exploring the state. He also had an affinity for assaulting women.

On October 3rd, 1966, Eckard raped a woman in her apartment. She'd been doing some cleaning when he slipped a cord around her neck and garroted her to unconsciousness. She awakened as he was tearing her clothes off. Eckard plead guilty the following April of 1967, and was sentenced to just five years probation by Judge Howard F. Thompson, his lenient sentence due in part to the opinion of the psychiatrists who examined him and pronounced him a "good risk." Thompson was also impressed by the fact Eckard had been receiving psychiatric treatment for several months.

Just a few months after his sentencing, on August 13th, 1967, Eckard's 46-year-old mother, Maria, went for a short drive. She stopped in the desert near 36th Street and Shea Boulevard. She hooked up a hose from her vacuum cleaner to the tailpipe of her car, ran it through the car window, and killed herself with the carbon monoxide emissions.

Barely over a month later on September 16th, Danny Lee found himself wanting for money to help his married girlfriend in Mexico obtain a divorce and move to Arizona. Apparently unwilling to put his skills to use earning it legally, and having experience in overpowering unsuspecting women, he opted to kidnap a teenage girl for ransom money. It was around midnight when he approached pretty, brunette 18-year-old Donna Mae Place as she walked along 32nd Street and shoved her into a ditch. Eckard strangled her with a rope until she lost consciousness. When she regained her senses, Eckard slapped her and warned her to be quiet. Eckard used his shirt to gag the terrified woman as he walked her to a house on the corner of Citrus Way.

Eckard tied Donna up, shoving her into a white convertible, and headed onto the Black Canyon Highway northbound. A Highway Patrolman, Ellis Salyer, began pursuing the speeding vehicle. He was soon joined by Sgt. Frank Bond. As the pair fled, Eckard leaned over and removed Donna's gag. When she asked if he planned to kill her, he said he wouldn't, but that he would ransom her for the $500 he needed.

Sometimes topping 100 miles an hour, Eckard left the pavement near New River. He took a dirt road - likely what is now Table Mesa Road - east for several miles into the New

River Mountains. As they drove, Donna told Danny Lee, "If you pray, God might give you another chance." Danny Lee had an odd concept of the second chance God might give; in a note left later for his father, he wrote about his faith in God, and said it was because of God he got away that night. Apparently Eckard thought God, like certain members of the public, was rooting for him.

At an old mine in the desert about nine miles east of the Black Canyon Highway, Eckard abandoned the car, leaving Donna as he took off on foot. When officers reached the car, they were surprised to find Donna still tied up inside. It was the first anyone knew that a kidnapping had occurred.

Sgt. Frank Bond had grown up on the T-Ranch on Table Mesa Road and still lived in New River. His wife, June Evans Bond, was the daughter of one of the early owners of the once-vast cattle ranch. Few people knew the area better, but Eckard had a good head start by the time the officers cleared the vehicle and began a proper search. Searchers worked late into the night on the 17th until the dense cholla cactus and rugged terrain forced them to discontinue their efforts. They didn't find Eckard that night. The search intensified.

It wasn't the only major manhunt going on at the time. On September 18th, one of Arizona's most notorious criminals, Gary Tison, overpowered a prison guard, James Stiner, who was taking Tison to court. Wrestling Stiner's gun away, Tison shot and killed the guard. None other than legendary lawman and prison warden Frank Eyman led the search for Tison. Eyman had cemented his place in Arizona history over 35 years earlier when, as a Tucson police officer, he arrested elusive mobster John Dillinger in 1934.

During the exhaustive searches in the desert, law enforcement and corrections officials were taxed to their fullest.

One prison staffer, Deputy Warden Leo H. Hochstatter, spent nearly twenty consecutive hours searching for Tison. On his return to regular duty, he collapsed and died of a massive heart attack. It was a brutal week for Eyman and his prison staff.

Once Tison was captured near Casa Grande, resources were immediately diverted to assist in the hunt for Eckard. Soon the manhunt involved over 70 men, many on horseback, supported by bloodhounds, posse members, and aircraft. Prison guards participated as well. It had been under Warden Eyman's watch that Eckard, like Tison, had made his escape. Eyman was a no-nonsense type and doubtless took it personally when escapes happened.

Still, Eckard stayed ahead of the searchers, sometimes by just seconds. A friend, Leo Gardner, helped Eckard out by providing food, new boots, and other essentials. Even though law enforcement officers kept an eye on Gardner's home on E. St. John Road, a few blocks north of Bell Road, they missed Eckard by less than a minute on one occasion.

At night, Eckard roughed it. He slept in the desert mountains most of the time. On September 22nd, though, he carefully broke into a model home, one of the typical low-slung ranch homes popular at the time, in the typically-named subdivision of "Paradise Sands," at 2443 E. Acoma. There, he enjoyed a night of relative luxury. When he left the next morning, he replaced the window glass he'd removed, but took a blanket and pillows with him.

Six days later, weary of being on the run, sensitive to the stress his situation was causing his father, and well aware of the precarious position he was putting his friends in, Eckard called police from Gardner's house. Two sergeants from Maricopa County Sheriff's Office, Don Golding and Harry Koch, responded to the St. John address. Eckard gave himself up without incident. He willingly talked about his tactics and survival methods.

Eckard might not have been so casual had he realized he could potentially face the death penalty for the kidnapping he'd committed. As it was, he was sentenced to 85 - 100 years after the probation revocation for the 1966 rape was combined with his more recent convictions. He faced the likelihood of never tasting freedom again.

That, however, would not be Eckard's fate. Despite his aptitude and inclination for escape, he was granted the opportunity to participate in a work gang on the prison ranch. On June 21, 1968, Danny Lee Eckard embarked on his second flight from justice.

Warden Eyman believed in rehabilitation and in giving inmates jobs outside the prison walls to relieve the tedium of incarceration. Danny Lee Eckard was the beneficiary of that policy. In the full heat of summer, he walked away from the prison work gang. He made it through miles of the flat, harsh desert between Florence and Apache Junction and promptly stole a car. On July 2nd, while - in the aftermath of Bobby Kennedy's assassination - much of the nation focused on another woman by the same name, Eckard abducted a 20-year-old student nurse named Joan Kennedy.

At about noon, young Joan, after picking up her mail, was followed by Eckard into her Sunnyslope-area apartment at 6116 N. 12th Place. He was armed with a .357 revolver. Using the same tactics he had in the past with his female victims, Eckard gagged and tied Joan up. A creature of habit, he had once again gravitated to the general area he'd lived in - despite the statewide search for him. He took Joan in her own car on a road trip she'd never forget. Once again, he'd head to the desert mountains north of Phoenix.

Eckard stopped in the fairly new master-planned community of Carefree to fuel up before taking the Black Canyon Highway to the Bumblebee road. While they drove, he opened up to Joan about who he was and how he'd eluded searchers. Referring to himself as "the Fox," he vowed not to go back to prison. As he had been with Donna Mae Place, Eckard was polite to Kennedy. He described how, when officers near Florence were close on his trail, he'd walked backwards in his own footprints and climbed a tree to hide as they passed beneath him. About five hours after her ordeal began, Joan Kennedy was released physically unscathed at the Crown King campground in the Bradshaw Mountains.

Eckard demonstrated concern for Joan's welfare, letting her take her car, giving her directions to get back to the Black Canyon Highway, and assuring her she'd have enough gas to do so. Joan was able to make her way back to the paved road and report the kidnapping. Eckard fled on foot into the mountains. The temperature reached 109 in Phoenix that day. In the Bradshaws it would be cooler, but with the monsoons already underway, Eckard would face the violent mountain storms.

Monsoons in the Bradshaws can be deadly. They bring lightning, torrential rain, and flash flooding. For Eckard, it brought the opportunity to elude the searchers who converged on Horse Thief Basin. The heavy rains prevented the bloodhounds from following his scent. One newspaper account pointed out that even the weather was on Danny Lee's side. Still, the forested mountains weren't Eckard's chosen turf. Managing to survive the busy July 4th holiday in the mountains without being caught, the next day he dropped back to the lower elevation of Black Canyon City.

The Highway Patrol, ever a thread woven through Eckard's life, worked a busy holiday. Between searching for the fugitive, handling the heavy traffic the holiday reliably brings to the state's highways, and responding to typical weather-related traffic incidents, they were among the emergency personnel responding to seven traffic fatalities over the weekend. In Tonto Basin, law enforcement and Civil Air Patrol were among the searchers who spent four days searching for lost middleweight boxer Jimmy Martinez before a Tonto National Forest helicopter, returning from fighting a forest fire, spotted him and his puppy in a ravine. Martinez had been fishing with friends at Hell's Hole Pond when he became separated and lost. A helicopter from Williams AFB ultimately carried Martinez and his pup to safety. Just about everything that emergency services could respond to, they responded to that July 4th week in 1968, and just about everyone involved in emergency services was put to work.

It was a Highway Patrolman flagged down by Joan Kennedy who escorted her back to Phoenix, and it was Highway Patrolmen who'd continue chasing Eckard's tail and trail back and forth from the state's central mountains to the valley below. On Friday, July 5th, Eckard stealthily made his way into Black Canyon City.

Sylvia McDonald, living at the time at the end of Kiva Road, was babysitting little Shauna Lee Clements when she heard her dogs barking. She told me she'd gone out to investigate. "I caught this guy out milking the cows," she said. "When he saw me, he took off across the river and to the little pink house across from Coldwater. Roger and Sue Wagner lived there with the kids. He kidnapped Sue and the kids at gunpoint. They were just itty bitty toddlers."

Suzanne Wagner was nineteen years old, pregnant, and already a mother of two. With her in the house at Coldwater Creek and River Bend Road were one-year-old Roger Jr. and two-year-old Shelly. Suzanne had been asleep when Eckard, a .357 Colt Python revolver in hand, awakened her in the bedroom and told her, "It's time to get up." Eckard, by now an expert at kidnapping, was calm and decisive; Sue, like previous abductees, described him as "almost gentle." Telling Suzanne to get dressed and get the kids ready, he refilled his canteens and helped himself to a Coca-Cola while he waited. Suzanne had time to fix a bottle for her little boy as Eckard told her where he'd been the past few days.

Eckard headed back to Phoenix in Suzanne's car with Suzanne and the children. Although worried for her children, Suzanne later said they seemed to be fond of Eckard. Sue noticed how tired he was, and how carefully he drove to avoid drawing attention to the vehicle. Once again, predictably, Eckard made his way back to his old stomping grounds in Sunnyslope. At 12th Street and Northern, Eckard came to a stop. He didn't say anything to the young woman and children but silently grabbed his pack and simply walked away.

Suzanne immediately headed to her aunt's home just blocks away near N. 4th Street but, finding the house unoccupied, contacted neighbors across the street. From their home, Suzanne called police. She knew, of course, it was Eckard, and they responded immediately. Within minutes, they saturated the area. Eckard, who'd headed westbound for the canal, took cover in an oleander grove. Despite the gun in his hand, he gave himself up without a struggle when patrol officers Robert W. Patty and Jerry Miller directed him to come out.

Facing the patrolmen aiming weapons at him, Eckard dropped the gun as commanded. Photos of him being taken into custody show a gaunt, raw-boned man in handcuffs, his hair cropped short, in his socks in the 100-degree heat as a Phoenix officer holds his cowboy boots and guides him toward the transport vehicle. This time, he'd had fifteen days of freedom. He'd kidnapped four people, stolen cars, roamed the mountains and the urban neighborhoods, milked cows, and survived hot weather, thunderstorms, and blowing dust.

Near the Arizona Canal, where Eckard had been recaptured, he'd cached and carefully camouflaged some useful items - among them, a cordless razor, boxes of ammunition, someone else's credit card, a half dozen cans of soup and - ever faithful - a St. Christopher medal. Eckard, the survivor, was prepared as always.

For months after his return to the Florence prison Eckard would be kept in segregation and any privileges withheld. In March of 1969, the restrictions were lifted and he was allowed to go back to general population, including having access to the outdoors exercise yard.

Just two months later, Eckard climbed the thirteen-foot fence around the Arizona State Prison yard. Unseen by the guards posted in towers at corners of the yard, he slipped off into the 100 degree heat of late May. Again, Frank Eyman personally led the search, deploying every available prison guard to look for Eckard. Eyman warned the public this time that Eckard was more dangerous now, a desperate man who'd be more likely to violently resist. Road blocks were established. Law enforcement officers in Florence saturated the area, checking personally on residents out of concern Eckard would hold locals hostage.

In South Vietnam, U.S. troops were fighting and dying on Dong Ap Bia - the mountain infamously called, "Hamburger Hill." In Seattle, students rioted, and across the nation, people followed the progress of Apollo 10's eight day voyage. In Arizona, many of us were focused on Eckard's latest exploits, and we were wary. I had just turned six years old four days earlier, but I remember my parents wouldn't let me go outside to play. Dad told me the "Desert Fox," was again on the loose and might be in the area.

Despite his relative proximity, our paths didn't cross Eckard's. He kept a low profile his first three days on the loose, but at eleven a.m. on May 27th, he surprised a woman at her new home on Hitching Post Road in Apache Junction and demanded the keys to her white four-door car. The woman, Jeanette Lake, was fortunate. Eckard didn't take her with him. In typical fashion, he reassured the woman he wouldn't harm her, and told her to quit shaking. Jeanette asked him what he'd do in her situation and he admitted he'd probably shake, too, but that he had problems of his own right now.

After taking some food and a pair of Mr. Lake's shoes, Eckard drove the Lake's car to Canyon Lake, a reservoir formed by Mormon Flat Dam off the Apache Trail, and fled on foot into that famously rugged terrain. It was located there in a parking lot near the dam by 3:15 in the afternoon, but despite intensive search efforts including air support, Eckard was not to be found. Like the coyotes in the Arizona desert, he seemed to just vanish into the brush and sand within seconds of a sighting.

Two days later, on Thursday, May 29th, Eckard returned to Apache Junction to steal another vehicle. This time he chose a Toyota Land Cruiser. He nearly made it through the Memorial Day weekend without incident, but at noon on Monday, June 2nd, an observant citizen reported a suspicious, shirtless man driving a Land Cruiser near Cave Creek Road. The Maricopa County deputy who responded, Andy Velasquez, made a stop on the car just south of New River Road. Velasquez turned his back on Eckard as he walked back to his patrol car. Eckard called out to the deputy to stop, and when Velasquez turned around, Eckard had a .45 aimed at him. As drivers passed by and watched, Velasquez stood in the unenviable position of hands up and a gun aimed at his chest. Rather than shoot, Eckard elected to disarm the deputy and handcuff him to the door handle of the patrol car. He took Velasquez' .357 and fled in the Land Cruiser.

Velasquez remained cuffed to the car in the full sun until a motorist finally stopped. Using a handcuff key of his own, the citizen freed the uninjured, but certainly embarrassed, deputy. Unsurprisingly, from there Eckard returned to the area he was most familiar with. Trackers followed his trail to the area of 12th and Northern. That neighborhood was a magnet to Eckard. Also unsurprisingly, officers found another of his campsites and supplies caches nearby, hidden in a box near the home of Bishop Joseph M. Harte at 815 E. Orangewood. Eckard had stashed canned food, more ammunition, a .22 handgun, and other necessities. At the time, there was a large orange grove on Orangewood, offering Eckard concealment and much-needed shade.

The following day another Eckard camp was found, this time at a cave near New River. Apparently growing wise to the pattern Eckard had established of continually returning to favorite spots, officers visited the area where he'd released Donna Mae Place in the New River Mountains. They found tracks they believed to be from the stolen Land Cruiser, and a sleeping bag inside the cave - but Danny had again slipped away.

By now the media was finding Eckard's prolonged escape amusing. Paul Dean, the *Arizona Republic's* wry and beloved columnist, noted that the paper's photographer had an excellent suggestion for finding the Fox. Earl McCartney, one of the army of newsmen responding to points along Eckard's trail, noted wryly to a deputy, "Tell all your guys to keep quiet. Then you'll be able to hear Danny laughing." Recent descriptions of Eckard in the paper were grimly amusing as well: By now they included mention of his sunburned face, the skin peeling, and his chapped lips.

Eckard worked his way north to the cool country. A week after his encounter with Deputy Velasquez, Eckard resurfaced at a summer home in Groom Creek in the Bradshaw Mountains. A Phoenix couple, Dennis and Pat Hill, were enjoying a respite from the heat at their cabin when Eckard approached Pat at about ten a.m. He tied her to a chair and, gun in hand, searched for her husband. No sooner had Dennis greeted the stranger then he found himself at gunpoint. Dennis, too, was promptly tied up to a chair near his wife. As usual, Eckard was polite and showed concern for his victims, asking them for information about who he should call to come release them after he got out of the area. He loosened the ropes when the Hills told him they were tied too tightly. As a result, they were able to free themselves within just ten minutes or so after Eckard had driven off in their 1969 white Ford pickup truck.

Dennis Hill immediately phoned police. Dispatchers alerted law enforcement throughout the area, notifying Highway Patrol officers, Game and Fish Rangers, and county deputies. Yavapai County Deputy Sheriff Lionel B. "Gil" Gilpin was the first to catch sight of Eckard headed northbound on U.S. 89. As Gilpin passed through Chino Valley, he picked up two Game and Fish officers, Harley Shaw and Miles Rohda. Eckard realized he was being tailed and doubled back, but he didn't lose the officers. The pursuit picked up speed and size as more officers flocked to the area. Officers Paul Marston and Ronald Mayes and Yavapai County Lieutenant Jack Findley were soon on scene.

Above: Four Winds Farm as it appears in 2018. The original barn and the arched building to the left appear as they did when Eckard used them as cover.

Eckard turned onto Perkinsville Road and pulled into Four Winds Farm. Now cornered, he stopped the pickup truck just to the left of a building. To the right of the building stood a large barn, open on both ends. Eckard ran from the truck and out of view behind the long, narrow building beside it. As Officer Marston rushed into the clearing, shotgun in hand, Eckard came around the building from the other side, near the barn. He shot

Marston with the .357 magnum he'd taken from Deputy Velasquez the week before.

Eckard picked up Marston's shotgun. As Harley Shaw rushed towards the critically injured Marston, Eckard shot him. Shaw, wounded in the hand, arm, and head, was out of the battle. As he exited his car, Lt. Findley took a hit. Although wounded in the pelvic area, he staggered back to the patrol car to call for assistance. Ron Mayes, still in the Highway Patrol car, had already radioed that Marston was down. Seeing Shaw get hit, he got him into the car for cover.

Despite the running gun battle, Eckard managed to catch a horse to use for cover as he fled toward the barn. Entering it from the back, he bolted out the front towards the remaining officers, gun blazing. By the time Ron Mayes and Deputy Sheriff Gilpin returned fire, Eckard was directly in front of the car. Mayes, taking cover behind the open door of the patrol car, shot above the door. Mayes then ducked down and shot from beneath the car door. Eckard responded by running around the front of the car to the opposite side. At that point Mayes stood up, stretched across the patrol car roof, and shot directly at Eckard's head. One bullet penetrated the center of Eckard's forehead, taking a chunk of his skull when it exited. The Desert Fox fell backwards, his final escape at an end, bleeding profusely into the dust.

Both Marston and Eckard were transported to the Emergency Room at Yavapai Community Hospital. Neither regained consciousness. There, an hour apart and just feet away, they were each pronounced dead, the good guy and the bad guy.

Above: Paul Edward Marston, Arizona Highway
Patrolman. End of watch: June 9, 1969.

Just shy of 31 years old, Paul Marston, badge number 138, was the first Arizona Highway Patrolman to be shot and killed, and only the second Highway Patrol officer to be killed in the line of duty. Hundreds, including warden Frank Eyman, paid their respects at his funeral. Marston was laid to rest in

Mountain View Cemetery in Prescott. His children were but three and four years old. Among those contributing to a fund for the family was businessman Tom Chauncey, for whom I later worked.

At Danny Lee Eckard's funeral, Reverend Howard Hart of Sunnyslope Baptist Church presided over services attended by about sixty people. Two years earlier he'd performed services at the funeral of Danny's mother, Maria. Eckard's military-funded casket was covered with a U.S. flag in honor of his years of service as a Marine. In a second grotesque tribute, a month after his burial, Eckard's father, Rupert, received a letter from President Richard M. Nixon stating, "The United States honors the memory of Danny L. Eckard. This certificate is awarded by a grateful nation in recognition of devoted and selfless consecration to the service of our country in the Armed Forces of the United States." Columnist Paul Dean, disgusted by the accolades (while nonetheless recognizing they were automatically issued anytime a veteran died), wrote that Eckard's uncle, Robert Myers, said, "When you get your guts torn out over something like this, it really means something when you get a letter like this."

Some of the public also still mourned the cop-killing Eckard. One letter to the editor of the *Arizona Republic* bemoaned the "excessive" sentence given to him for the rapes and kidnappings he'd committed, rationalizing that he'd been driven to kill because he'd been tragically deprived of all hope. A staffer at Yavapai Community Hospital wrote to reassure the public that every effort had been made to save Eckard's life, angry that Paul Dean had previously written about anger being directed at Eckard for the death of Marston. Questions arose, astonishingly enough, about the necessity of shooting Eckard. Little has changed since then. The lines between hero and villain have, and probably always will, be blurred in the cognitive dissonance of the popular imagination.

In 1992, 23 years after Eckard's death, yet another survival-oriented convict escaped from the prison in Florence. His 54-day self-granted furlough evoked memories of Eckard. The convict, a convicted armed robber who kidnapped people and stole cars during his summer vacation on the run, was named Danny Ray Horning. Reporters who recalled the earlier escapee Danny contacted Officer Ron Mayes, who'd shot Eckard, for his insight. Mayes described how Eckard had conditioned himself for his escape while still in prison, doing daily push-ups, and how he had breathed through reeds while underwater in the canal to escape detection, ridden cows, and run backwards "for miles" to leave footprints in the wrong direction. Chillingly, Mayes said he'd later learned Eckard had planned an epic final showdown in the Mohave desert in which he'd lure officers after him and then shoot down each tired pursuer one at a time.

Whether or not Eckard had such plans or even used such escape tactics may have been clouded by memory and human inclination to exaggeration. Certainly he inspired other convicts, some members of the media, and certain elements of the public with his exploits.

In December, 1971, two inmates from Arizona State Prison at Florence concealed themselves in a truck full of newly-minted license plates made by prisoners. They were strangely connected to Eckard. One was a convicted murderer named Anthony Kozlinski, who'd killed a man in Black Canyon City; the other, 26-year-old Charles Blevins, was Danny Lee Eckard's brother-in-law. Blevins was quoted in the *Arizona Republic* as having told someone he would make Eckard "look like a piker."

Aftermath and Author's Notes

Prison Warden Frank Eyman lived a big life. He died on June 13, 1984 after a 52 year career in law enforcement. In 1950, after serving 20 years as a Tucson Police Officer in positions ranging from patrol, detective, and assistant chief, Eyman retired and was elected as Pima County Sheriff. The local press welcomed him to the office by describing him as having qualifications "unmatched in the nine-man field and, for that matter, unsurpassed by any candidate in the recent history of the county." Eyman would continue to serve as sheriff for three terms. Eyman's service to the state's law enforcement officers continues even today: he is responsible for bringing the Fraternal Order of Police to Arizona. The FOP Lodge Eyman founded was in Tucson, which is why it is Arizona's FOP Lodge #1. According to my longtime fellow FOP member John Barto, "When Eyman is mentioned at state FOP functions, he is always referred to as our beloved Frank Eyman."

As a young man, Eyman served as a Fifth Cavalry horse soldier during World War I. During his illustrious career he had also served as a special agent for a midwestern railroad, followed by tenure at Southern Pacific Railroad in Arizona; chief criminal investigator for the Office of Naval Intelligence at Pearl Harbor; provost marshal for the Navy prison at Terminal Island, California; and warden of the Arizona State Prison from 1955 to 1972. A lawman of the old school, Eyman once attracted perhaps valid criticism for welding shut the cell doors of nearly 100 prisoners who'd rioted and refusing to feed them, but he had the respect of the prisoners for his fairness. He adamantly supported many paroles and, like the early wardens of the Yuma Territorial Prison, encouraged rehabilitation efforts.

Arizona-born Deputy Sheriff Lionel B. "Gil" Gilpin died at age 88 in Paulden.

Donna Mae Place, taken hostage by Eckard in 1967, married two years later.

On June 3, 1969, the dispatcher who'd broadcast the suspicious subject call to Deputy Andy Velasquez resigned after being given a five-day suspension. Sheriff's department staff disciplined Darrell McCloud for failing to caution Velasquez the subject was possibly Eckard. McCloud said he didn't want to fence the inevitable calls from the media if he said the name, "Eckard," but that he also didn't want officers becoming complacent if the dispatchers repeatedly used the name when dispatching.

Game and Fish biologist Harley Shaw recovered from his wounds and continued on to a lengthy and widely respected tenure at the agency. Shaw, who moved to New Mexico after retirement, has written several books on wildlife and game management.

It is said there are still bullet holes visible in the barn at Four Winds Ranch in Chino Valley. At the time of the shooting, the racehorse facility was one of the largest ranches in the area. Today, the barn and ranch still stand, looking largely the same as it did at the time of Paul Marston's death.

In the 1990s, while I was stationed as a Basic Training Lieutenant at the Arizona Law Enforcement Academy, an enthusiastic, cheerful young man came on board as a recruit training officer while he recovered from a serious on-duty motorcycle accident. Following in his father's footsteps, he was a DPS officer - Highway Patrol. He looked strikingly like his father. His name was Brian Marston.

Retelling the Danny Lee Eckard story thus has some personal significance for me. From that first warning from my father about the Desert Fox being on the loose again, to a gradual awareness of a certain mythos that developed around him, I grew up with the awareness of Eckard. Although I'd followed the story of Eckard's escapes as they happened, I used numerous newspaper archives in my research including articles from the *Arizona Republic,* the *Tucson Daily Citizen*, the *Palm Springs (California) Desert Sun*, and others.

Sylvia McDonald graciously provided her first-hand account of seeing Danny Lee Eckard at her family's home in Black Canyon City, as well as sharing what she knew of his local exploits.

In researching my book, *Images of America: New River,* I had the good fortune of interviewing and becoming friends with June Evans Bond. June had spoken at length of her late husband, Frank Bond, who was involved in the search in the New River Mountains for Danny Lee Eckard.

Site visits include the Four Winds Farm in Chino Valley.

The illustration at the beginning of this chapter is my original linocut block print depicting the barn at Four Winds Farm in Chino Valley.

Chapter 9

A Go-Go Girl, A Serviceman, and a Mine Shaft

The Murder of Sgt. Lawrence Broughall

Larry Broughall must have sensed something was going down. The Vietnam veteran had recently bought a revolver for self-protection and on December 2, 1969, he was carrying it. That night, he'd gotten a call from his ex-girlfriend, a young but already hardened go-go dancer, asking if he could give her and her teenage sister a ride to Mesa to see their dad. Despite having broken up with Donna Louise Smith, the Air Force sergeant picked up Donna and her 16-year-old sister Shirley in Cashion. Broughall, a Vietnam veteran who'd been assigned to Luke Air Force Base since his return the previous year, set the .22 pistol down next to him and headed off to give the girls a lift.

Broughall had poor taste in women. Donna was a blue-eyed blonde who'd moved to Phoenix the year before. She and her father had come from California, but their relationship was troubled. By the time she dated Broughall, she'd already been married, had separated in just a month, divorced, and had attempted suicide. More recently, she'd begun hanging around with a motorcycle gang who called themselves "The Devil's Diciples" (the "Diciples" claimed to deliberately misspell "Disciples" on the off chance of being confused with a religious group). Donna had been engaged to one of the members of the outlaw gang, Anthony Thomas "Tony" Kozlinski, although they'd broken the engagement. Although she later claimed she was clean the week before the ill-fated ride with Broughall, she'd been a heavy narcotics user, as was Kozlinski, and had recently helped her kid sister run away from home. She'd been busying herself lately doing armed robberies and, just three days after the ride with Broughall, she and another woman robbed a beauty salon and a liquor store. Donna was nineteen years old.

Her little sister, Shirley, was following in Donna's go-go-booted footsteps. Already she'd been deemed delinquent for participating in several crimes. As Broughall drove, Shirley and Donna told him they needed to stop to pee. Donna had a plan that involved more than peeing, and by the time Broughall pulled over in the desert around 99th Avenue and Buckeye Road, she had already put it into motion. She snatched his .22 off the seat and she and Shirley dashed into the darkness of the desert. Simultaneously, as had been prearranged, a car with four men in it pulled up. At gunpoint, the men yanked Broughall out of the car, pummeling him as they forced him onto the ground. As the girls returned, Broughall asked Donna why they were attacking him. Donna told him it was "payment." She felt he'd wronged her, somehow. She'd get even.

The men put the beaten 22-year-old into their car and one of them, a baby-faced 24-year-old named Kenneth Scarborough, drove Broughall's car. Scarborough, by some accounts the leader of the local chapter of the fledgling Diciples gang, made the lengthy drive to a dark, quiet area just west of Black Canyon City. They already knew where they were headed. The gang drove to the base of a hill and forced Broughall face down in the dirt. Shirley and Donna ransacked his car, clearing it of personal effects in an effort to conceal the identity of the owner, and the four attackers beat Broughall further. They took the cash he had on hand - a meager $31, and not the full amount of the paycheck they'd anticipated he'd just received - and tore a ring from his finger.

Broughall, already severely injured and agonizingly aware of his fate, was taken on a death march up the hill. At top was the entry to a vertical mine shaft. The newspaper accounts of the crime scene were vague; the hilltop shaft was about a mile west of Black Canyon City and 69 feet deep. The men positioned Broughall on the brink of the open shaft. It was nearly daybreak when 24-year-old former Army medic Anthony T. "Tony" Kozlinski, holding a .22 caliber revolver, allegedly asked who was going to kill Broughall. Kozlinski later testified Scarborough took the weapon from him, pointed it just above Broughall's left ear and shot him, then put the gun back into Kozlinski's hand. Gravity pulled Broughall's body unassisted into the mine shaft. The men joined the two teenage girls waiting by Broughall's car and set it on fire to further delay identification of their victim.

Broughall left behind four younger siblings and his parents, Geneva and James Broughall, in Jacksonville, Florida. It was several days before anyone from his family knew of his death. His body remained in the mine shaft until four days later, after Phoenix police detective Don Toms questioned Donna Louise Smith and her colleagues about a series of armed robberies. That Friday night, December 5th, Toms had taken Smith, her sister Shirley, another 16-year-old named Sharon Yvonne Davis, and Kenneth Scarborough in on charges of multiple counts of armed robbery and assault with a deadly weapon. During questioning, the suspects startled Toms by saying there had possibly been a murder - and that they'd dumped the body into a mineshaft. Toms immediately stopped the questioning and notified the proper agency, Yavapai County Sheriff's Office, who had jurisdiction over the homicide case.

The following day, Yavapai County officers successfully retrieved Broughall's body from the mine shaft. One of Broughall's colleagues from the 58th Field Maintenance squad, Sgt. Smith Young, identified the body. Sgt. Young had been one of the last of Broughall's squadron mates to see him alive, just as Broughall finished his shift at 4:15 p.m. on December 1st.

In connection to the murder investigation, nine people were initially taken into custody. Of them, Tony Kozlinski, Donna Louise Smith, Sharon Yvonne Davis, and Kenneth Scarborough resided in the same apartment - number 128 - at 2219 W. Devonshire in Phoenix. Ultimately, five of the nine were charged with Broughall's murder. In addition to the elder Smith sister, Kozlinski, and Scarborough, two Canadians, 17-year-old Keith Roland Olsen and 20-year-old Dennis Leon Martel, were also charged. The Canadians nearly made it to the border in their car (bearing Canadian plates) before being stopped by a vigilant Nebraska State Trooper in North Platte, Nebraska.

Throughout the investigation and the ensuing criminal trial, the suspects' accounts of their motives for the crime varied. Donna Louise Smith variously claimed she'd feared Broughall would tell authorities she was harboring her runaway sister; that when joyriding with the men from the gang, they asked her if there was anyone she wanted to rob or kill, and she gave Broughall's name because of "things he'd done to her;" and that they were simply looking for someone to rob, so she nominated him.

During the investigation and ensuing trials, Donna was forthright about accepting responsibility for the murder. According to newspaper accounts, during the trial she tearfully admitted saying, "Go ahead, snuff him. I don't care," during the assault on Broughall. She testified against Scarborough during his separate trial, but confessed to her court-ordered lawyer that she was responsible for "the entire mess" and wanted to "take the entire blame for the whole thing." It was clear Donna had orchestrated the brutal, senseless crime.

Broughall's grieving mother, 40-year-old Geneva, silently attended the trial of Kenneth Scarborough. Few of the attendees at the trial knew she was present. After hearing the jury's decision to acquit Scarborough, Mrs. Broughall told reporter John Fuhrman of the *Arizona Republic* she came to the trial so she could know who pulled the trigger, not for "revenge or hatred."

On July 1, 1970, the tall, red-haired, red-mustached Tony Kozlinski received a sentence of three to five years on a charge of aggravated battery for his part in the armed robbery. Following his sentencing, Donna Louise Smith pleaded with the judge to perform a marriage service for her and Kozlinski. The judge, Jack Ogg, refused to do so until the entire Broughall case had been adjudicated. Adding insult to injury, Tony Kozlinski also refused to participate, telling his attorney he did not want to be married at that juncture in his life. Apparently one lengthy sentence was enough. Donna, however, cried at the loss of such a charming partner. Kozlinski was later sentenced to ten to 20 years for the murder of Broughall. Even prison would not keep him from trouble.

The prison in Florence, built as the shiny new replacement for the old Yuma Territorial Prison, wasn't pleasant. By the close of 1969, it was still the only state prison facility and was woefully overcrowded. Designed for 805 adults, it housed 1,665, and officials readily acknowledged that some of the facilities were worthy of condemnation.

On September 23, 1970, Donna tearfully received her sentence of 15 years to life for her part in Broughall's death. She would become inmate #30063 at the Arizona Department of Corrections. Her kid sister Shirley was sent to a school for delinquent girls, The Bunkhouse in the Bradshaws, in Crown King. There, the teenager who'd already assisted in the murder of a man would be housed in an unlocked dormitory and provided classes in beauty, hygiene, sewing, and crafts. Her spare time would be spent doing sing-a-longs and writing letters.

It wasn't just the girls in Donna's extended family who grew up to be violent offenders. On June 24, 1970, at only 15, Donna's stepbrother Mark "Angel" Foust shot a 19-year-old Paradise Valley youth, Mario Richardson, killing him in an act as brutally unnecessary as Broughall's murder. Foust, a sixth-grade dropout known to openly wear a gun he dubbed, "Suzy," frightened the people who knew him. One night while Angel and his longtime friend, 17-year-old David Boshears, were hitchhiking at Central and McDowell in Phoenix, Richardson picked them up in his red '68 Camaro. Angel and David told him they wanted to go to a barbecue they'd heard about at the Verde River. Richardson, who had never met the boys before, complied. Richardson was anything but a troublemaker himself; at 5'7" he'd learned he was too short to be a police officer as he'd dreamed, but had enlisted in the Navy and at the end of summer was slated to leave for training.

When they reached an isolated spot off Fort McDowell Road near the river, Foust used the same ruse Donna had used, telling Richardson he needed to go to the bathroom. Richardson stopped not far from the Phoenix-owned Verde Water Treatment Plant on county land near Red Mountain, east of Scottsdale. Before Foust returned to the car, Richardson indicated he was leaving. Foust shot him four times with a .22 revolver, striking him in the arm, leg, and twice in the head as Richardson tried desperately to make it back inside his car. Foust dragged the body about twenty feet from the dirt road. Richardson's body was found with no identifying clues save for a necklace with "Mario" and "Love, Mary," - Mario's girlfriend - inscribed on it.

Foust and Boshears left in Richardson's Camaro, abandoning it in central Phoenix. Angel, a frequent drug abuser, later claimed he was under the influence of LSD. His defense witnesses included psychologists who, unsurprisingly, described him as exhibiting sociopathic tendencies.

Angel Foust had his own interaction with members of the Devil's Diciples shortly thereafter. On July 22nd, Angel shot and critically wounded the vice-president of the local Devil's Diciples chapter, 24-year-old William "Cowboy" Topping, with a shotgun. Foust was again accompanied by his curly-haired blonde friend Boshears as well as two downtown-Phoenix friends, William S. Gadd and Stephen Cooper. While westbound on Roosevelt at about one a.m., the teens, with Gadd at the wheel of the 1956 Plymouth, noticed a motorcycle with two riders pull up beside them at a red light. Gadd claimed to recognize one of the riders as "Red," who was allegedly responsible for the death of a friend in California the year before. Boshears later testified that Gadd prompted Foust to use the sawed-off 12 gauge double-barrel shotgun in the car and shoot "Red." Gadd passed the gun to Foust, in the back seat, and repeatedly directed him to shoot the biker. Foust took aim and shot Cowboy Topping - who was driving - in the back, causing the bike to go down. The passenger, Kinnith "Spider" Nicholson, wasn't badly hurt, and later identified Angel as the shooter. Authorities were quick to assume the shooting was related to internal strife within the Diciples, and that Spider was the intended target, but the theory was quickly abandoned. The boys were arrested within days of the shooting. Foust again claimed he was under the influence of acid - and beer - when he committed the crime.

The assault marked Angel for retribution. Angel, the typical tough guy when he had gun in hand, begged not to be jailed in

Arizona for his crimes because he feared for his life. He believed the Devil's Diciples would make good on their threats to avenge Cowboy's shooting. In February, 1971, he told Superior Court Judge Irwin Cantor he'd heard there were members of the gang in prison in the state and they'd threatened to kill him if he was incarcerated in Arizona. Facing the judge, Angel was suddenly keenly motivated to make something of his life. Angel went on to tell the judge he'd like to be sentenced only to probation so he could return to school and learn to fly airplanes. He was, in what was apparently an act of mercy, sent to Preston School of Industry in Ione, California to serve a 10 - 20 year sentence. On Friday, July 27, 1972, at just 17 years old, Mark Byron "Angel" Foust was fatally stabbed in the stomach in the California juvenile correctional facility.

The investigation into Foust's death found no connection between the incident and his Arizona misdeeds. It was, perhaps, just another odd coincidence. Foust was buried in Greenwood Cemetery in Phoenix, the same cemetery where Danny Lee Eckard was interred.

In another such coincidence, on July 25, 1972, just two days before her stepbrother would be murdered, the ever-enterprising Donna Louise Smith, then 22 years old, escaped from prison. Along with a woman named Mary Brown and a not-so-trustworthy trusty named Leevend Hill, Smith slipped through a cut they made in the wire fence, climbed the exterior wall, and hopped a Los Angeles-bound Trailways Bus. When the trusty went into a restaurant at a bus stop in Dateland, near Yuma, a prison guard happened to recognize him and contact the Highway Patrol. The responding officer, Tim Fitch, arrested Hill and then located Donna on the bus. In yet another coincidence, a newspaper listed the death of Mark "Angel" Foust and the escape of Donna Louise Smith side by side in the same column of state briefs, making no connection between Donna and Angel.

As for the husband Donna had hoped to wed, Tony Kozlinski beat and sodomized a cellmate while being held in Maricopa County jail prior to his conviction. On December 21, 1971, Kozlinski and a 26-year old convicted armed robber, Charles Blevins, escaped from prison in Florence by hiding in crates of prison-made license plates loaded onto a truck. In one of the stranger side notes to the story of their escape, Charles Blevins was none other than the brother-in-law of Danny Lee Eckard.

After several weeks of freedom, on April 27, 1972, two deputies saw Kozlinski and Blevins in the company of two young women along Filter Plant Road near the Verde River in the same area where Angel Foust murdered Mario Richardson. While trying to apprehend them, the deputies - Steve Huntington and Bill Gaines - were captured at gunpoint by the shotgun-bearing fugitives. Kozlinski and Blevins handcuffed the deputies and, fortunately, chose to spare their lives. The two women, 15-year-old Janet Torok and 21-year old Susan Fullajtar - both from Connecticut - remained behind, wisely choosing not to be further involved, while the escapees fled in a car they'd stolen and kept at their campsite. Kozlinski and Blevins had met the women in Connecticut during their weeks of freedom, inexplicably returning to Arizona and bringing Torok and Fullajtar with them.

From there, Blevins and Kozlinski quickly took Paradise Valley resident Frank Anderson hostage. Near 96th Street and Cactus Road, an area known for its horse ranches, the fugitives flagged down Anderson in a manner worthy of a stagecoach robbery. As Anderson stopped his car for the gesturing fugitive, Blevins pointed a handgun at Anderson while Kozlinski, also armed, approached from the front. Taking their dark-blue stolen car with them, they directed Anderson to drive to his home, where they held him and his wife hostage for two days. On the second night of the ordeal, they snuck away in the Andersons' avocado green Chrysler sedan while the couple slept.

The two resourceful convicts headed northeast, making it 2,500 hundred miles before their journey's end. On May 6, the two were spotted by FBI agents at a Greenwich, Connecticut motel. The agents followed them, ultimately cornering them at the vacant Playland Amusement Park in Rye, New York. Kozlinski and Blevins opted for a shootout. They only managed to fire a couple of rounds before Blevins was hit by a shotgun round. In one of the many parallels with his brother-in-law Eckard, he died in a firefight with law enforcement after escaping prison at Florence. Tony Kozlinski was, once again, taken into custody. The two had shotguns, handguns, and nine rifles with them.

In 1974, psychiatrists were quoted in the paper as describing Kozlinski as "a master at hiding his alert mind behind a mask of imbecility, once attempting to escape from Arizona State Hospital by using a can of deodorant and some matches as a blow torch to get through a window." The account went on to say he'd told his doctors he continued to dream about his dead partner - Blevins - and that in the dreams Blevins beckoned him to "come over to the other side." The violence Kozlinski had chosen to surround himself with was finally paying dividends in post-traumatic stress.

Kozlinski was again returned to Florence, this time with a series of new charges. While incarcerated for four more concurrent sentences of 40 to life in addition to his 10 - 20 for murder, he again fled Florence. On October 2, 1975, now 29 years old, Kozlinski and a new traveling companion, Harmon Lee Ellis, were among a group of escapees. They stole a pickup truck and a .30-06 rifle from an area rancher, then took a string of hostages at rifle point. Hostage Ralph Gabardi's .32 revolver did him little good; Ellis and Kozlinski took it with them after forcing Gabardi to drive them to Glendale before being released, unharmed. They then took Evelyn Keogh hostage half a mile from where they'd been dropped off. The next day they took Richard Deal hostage, holding him in his trailer home on the west side of the valley. It was Deal's car they were driving when they were captured in Munds Park, south of Flagstaff. They were consistently friendly with their hostages, physically harming no one, Danny Lee Eckard style.

When the two were brought before Judge Howard Peterson for their latest crimes, the judge responded appropriately to the career criminals by giving them a 75 - 125 year sentence. They hurled profanities at him in a tirade questioning the harsh sentence, reasoning that others who'd "hurt people" only received five years' time. Ellis felt Peterson was "railroading" him into a life sentence in prison. He was, as it turns out, correct: on New Year's Eve, 1995, Ellis died in prison.

Kozlinski eventually made it back to Connecticut where he'd been raised. In a prisoner exchange, the Arizona Department of Corrections sent him to Somers State Prison. There, he continued his sociopathic tendencies. He and three other inmates were suspected, though never charged, with the strangulation death of Alfred T. Chisolm, a black inmate. As a result of the crime, the four were assigned to solitary confinement for four months. Kozlinski, ever assuming the victim mentality, felt persecuted by such treatment and initiated litigation against the Connecticut corrections authorities. He'd long since worn out his welcome. Connecticut wanted to send him back to Arizona. Kozlinski petitioned to stay in Connecticut, claiming the transfer was a vindictive response to his lawsuit and would disrupt his visitation rights. The judge, however, saw no merit to his appeals and ruled against him.

"Do the crime, do the time," was an unpopular sentiment with the bunch who murdered Lawrence Broughall. Escape was more their style. After pleading guilty to second-degree murder and aggravated battery in exchange for a reduced sentence, Canadian Dennis Leon Martel was granted the courtesy of serving his relatively brief sentence in the Yavapai County Jail instead of the Arizona State Prison at Florence. Martel, claiming he'd been badly beaten by prisoners at Florence for speaking about the Broughall case, was afraid they'd kill him if he had to serve his time there. Thanks to the recent legalization of a contract allowing such exceptions, Martel was granted the privilege of serving at the Yavapai jail. He was even made a trusty at the Yavapai jail. On January 26, 1971, Martel used an electric cord to descend the forty feet from the third floor of the jail kitchen to freedom. He'd decided to travel back to Manitoba to see his baby daughter for the first time. Martel made it as far as Kanab when a roadblock snared him. As a result of his escape, the contract to serve his time in the Yavapai jail was revoked. Martel was transferred back to Florence. His fears for his life notwithstanding, he survived.

Aftermath and Author's Notes

The biker shotgunned off his chopper, Cowboy Topping, ultimately recovered from his injuries, rode his bike on many more journeys, and went on to raise a family. He has since passed away.

Cowboy's passenger at the time of the shooting, and then-associate member of the Diciples, Texas-born Kinnith Ray "Spider" Nicholson, later distinguished himself by robbing a liquor store in drag. Spider shaved his legs, wore a "curly wig, lipstick, and a pullover sweater" and "carried a flowered handbag and a snub-nosed revolver," according to the September 20, 1970 *Arizona Republic*. Spider certainly had a unique flair for accessorizing. He was released early from his 25 year prison sentence in February, 1986. He died on October 24, 1988 in California, two years after his release.

Kenneth Scarborough, though acquitted of the murder of Lawrence Broughall, was convicted of the three-days-later robbery of Zeigler's Liquor Store in Mesa. He served time as prisoner #32507 and was released in 1976.

Donna Louise Smith was paroled on March 24, 1995. Her father, Rhees Smith, died in 1976, four years after his stepson "Angel" was killed and long before Donna would - legally, anyway - see freedom. Donna's mother, Rosetta, died in California within a year of Donna's release.

The kid sister, Shirley Smith, briefly served time as #32359 in the Arizona prison system after her time at the Bunkhouse school for delinquent girls.

The Devil's Diciples outlaw motorcycle club continues to be a national presence and in recent years has drawn significant attention from federal authorities for continued criminal activity.

One of the two Canadians convicted in the Broughall case, Dennis Leon Martel, died in Minnesota in April, 1984 just shy of his 35th birthday. He's buried in Roseau in the northern tip of the state, not far from his hometown of Sprague, just a few miles north side of the border.

The Verde Water Treatment Plant, built by Del Webb in 1948, closed in 2011 and has since been demolished.

I serendipitously happened across an article about the Broughall murder while researching other portions of this book. I had no memory of hearing of it prior to finding it in the newspaper stories of the time, but found it an irresistibly intriguing chapter in more recent Black Canyon history. As so many Black Canyon tales do, it touches on the larger history of Arizona. It is entirely drawn on research from newspaper archives and official records and documents.

A note on names: Anthony Kozlinski's name is spelled "Kozlinskie" on the Arizona Department of Corrections register. Dennis Martel's last name is spelled "Martell" on the register.

The illustration at the beginning of this chapter is an original linocut block print by the author depicting a .22 revolver, the caliber and type of gun used in Broughall's murder.

Chapter 10

A Finer Man You Couldn't Find

*Wild Bill Boady, the Midway Bar's Much-Loved Bartender
with the Ugly Past*

Hatchet, Kookie, Chico, Leg, and Jim were angry, and when they got angry, people were going to get hurt. The four tough guys, members of the Iron Cross outlaw biker gang in Pompano Beach, Florida, took umbrage at the fact a Puerto Rican man had run Jim off the road earlier in the day. Jim - whose full name was James Dale Purkhiser - and a few traveling companions pursued the man to a market at 18th Avenue and Hammondville Road, yelling threats they'd kill him. They didn't expect 20 fellow migrants to rise up and defend the man, Miguel Rivera, at the grocery store. The Puerto Rican laborers, some with makeshift cudgels in hand, jumped the knot of bikers and soundly beat them. Purkhiser even received a lump on the head.

Purkhiser withdrew from the one-sided fight and headed to the local Iron Cross clubhouse, a well-known neighborhood nuisance. There, Purkhiser rallied the support of his biker buddies. Seventeen of them, Hatchet and Kookie and Chico among them, went with him late that night to the local migrant worker camp, known as the "Pompano Beach Labor Camp." When the bikers, clad in their denim vests with a large "Iron Cross" graphic on the back, asked around, they were directed to a dwelling where Rivera was said to be living.

Chico carried a baseball bat. Kookie carried an axe. Purkhiser carried a .38 caliber semi-automatic given to him by Hubert Ray "Hatchet" Stidham of Fort Lauderdale. Hatchet, a sleepy-eyed 31 year old, joined Purkhiser, John Philemon "Kookie" Luke, and John Francis "Chico" Henry in barging into the house uninvited. Inside, they were met by a startled man named Luis Navarro. As they challenged Navarro in the living room, a disabled laborer, Tito Flores, emerged from his bedroom to find Navarro at gunpoint. When he asked what was going on he was greeted with gunshots.

The seven rounds fired didn't strike Tito. Instead, some struck Tito's 11-year-old daughter, Catalina, who was watching TV. Catalina cried out and dropped to the floor. The four bikers fled.

It was the wrong house. Miguel Rivera didn't live there. Little Catalina, nicknamed "Angel" for her sunny personality, died there.

It was 20 days before Christmas, 1965.

Until Catalina Flores' death, local authorities had looked at the Iron Cross bikers mostly as an annoyance. "This outfit is made up of misfits," one police officer told a reporter in 1966. When Catalina was killed, the community responded with understandable outrage. Over a dozen members of the gang were charged with various offenses related to the incident, most of them conspiracy to commit aggravated assault. Thirteen members were convicted. The man who pulled the trigger, Purkhiser, was convicted of first-degree murder and sentenced to the electric chair. Kookie, Chico, and Hatchet were convicted of third degree murder and sentenced to 20 years in prison.

In his own defense, Hatchet told reporters in 1966 that he was innocent and the bikers had never intended to kill anyone. By way of offering evidence, he said, "That's an insult to our mentality to think that we would go up there in a truck that couldn't go over 60 miles an hour to kill someone. I'm sure we had no business going up there but we didn't go looking for any trouble."

While the newly-convicted Hatchet was awaiting confinement pending appeal, the judge thought it a good idea to put a $3,000 bail on his head to hold him. In 1968, after losing the appeal, and facing decades in prison, Hatchet skipped town. He picked a place across country where he figured he'd blend in. Ultimately, he chose Black Canyon City, Arizona.

Black Canyon City was then a town of about 4,000 people. The Florida press would later describe it as "an isolated hamlet" in the mountains, with not even ten buildings in town. Hatchet reinvented himself. He ditched the motorcycle and adopted an area-appropriate interest in horses. He went completely bald and grew a distinctive handlebar mustache. He renamed himself, "Billy Ray Boady," and locals took to calling him, "Daddy Bill," or "Wild Bill" but they didn't see him as noticeably wild at all. For his first year in town, Daddy Bill lived with a woman who worked at mining camps across the region. Gloria Jean Moody's three sons looked at Daddy Bill as a father figure. Daddy Bill must have missed his own children, left behind in Florida in the care of his wife, Catherine Loraine.

Daddy Bill presented himself as a cowboy and a carpenter. He picked up work on the T-Ranch, cowboying, and did carpentry jobs around town. Gino Martin, then-owner of the Midway Bar, hired Daddy Bill as a bartender. Daddy Bill's popularity grew. "A finer man you couldn't find," Gino later said of Daddy Bill. The townspeople liked the way Daddy Bill helped them out, one-on-one, and many of them bonded with him across the bar at the Midway in the heart of town.

Despite calling himself a cowboy, there were signs Daddy Bill didn't know his way around a horse. Part of the ranch work

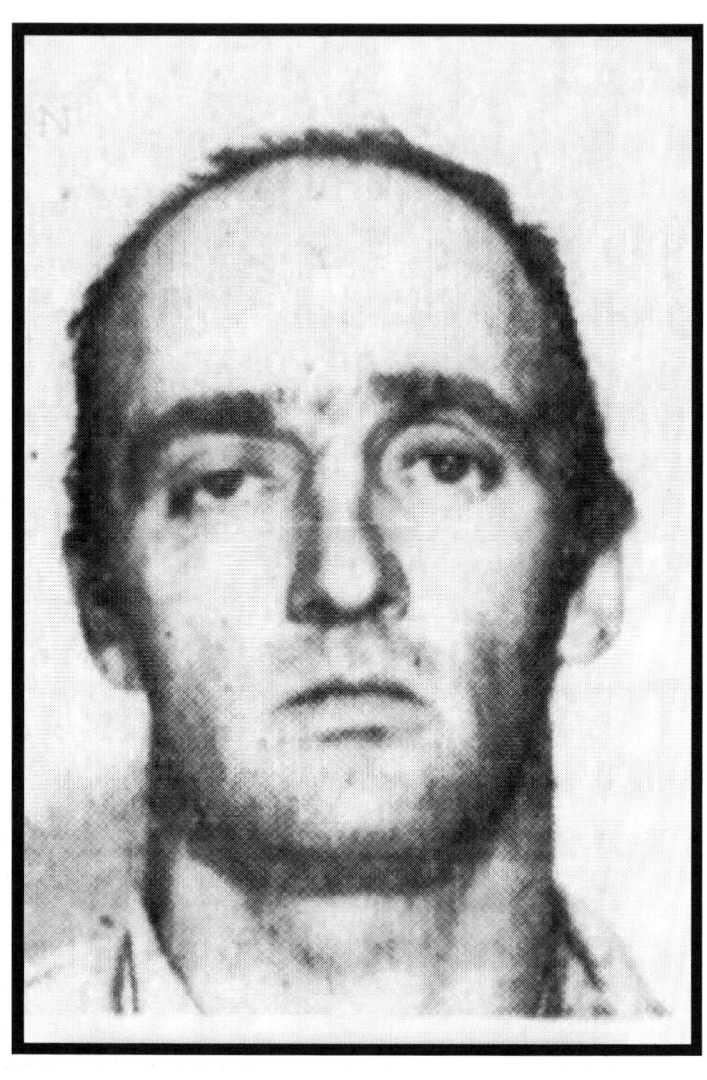

Above: Hubert Ray Stidham, aka "Daddy Bill Boady."

included leading pack strings into the rangeland with supplies needed by the livestock, such as salt blocks. Daddy Bill loaded a burro with six-packs of beer. The burro took offense to the way the pack rested and began to buck. Cans of beer shot out from the panniers, exploding as they struck the rocky ground. The burro bucked more with each popping can.

For most of his time in Black Canyon City, Daddy Bill lived in a trailer, quietly accruing a collection of long guns, shotguns, and handguns, as well as tack such as bridles and saddles. He took to accumulating Indian jewelry. He'd been there several years when, on August 7, 1974, Arizona FBI agents arrested him at the Midway Bar. The national papers noted he was armed at the time of his arrest. Daddy Bill had a tiny .22 caliber semi-automatic tucked into his pocket; locals were quick to point out it was but tradition to carry a gun in Black Canyon City.

Daddy Bill's friends were sympathetic. He'd changed, they believed. He was a truly good man. Gloria Jean Moody said that during his time living with her and her children, he'd cared for the boys. "My three boys think the world of Daddy Bill. I was away working in construction camps for weeks at a time and Billy Ray took care of them and the house. He cooked and baked and washed and ironed for them while I was gone," she told reporters. Daddy Bill's boss, Gino Martin, said, "There's not a woman or child that won't stand up and say they trust Daddy Bill anywhere anytime."

One-hundred-and-twenty townspeople signed a petition attesting to Daddy Bill's sterling character and pleading for leniency. They sent it with a delegate, Sandi Headrick, who carried it in person to Broward County and presented it to the judge, nearly nine years to the day after Catalina Flores' death. Catalina would have been twenty years old then, had she lived. The charitable people of Black Canyon City were willing to overlook the fact that Daddy Bill's gun, tack, and jewelry collection was burglarized entirely from their own homes - homes such as that of John Whitson of the Maggie Mine.

Daddy Bill - now Hubert Ray Stidham once again - wrote his own request for mercy. Papers described it as "barely literate," and mocked his spelling, such as the way he spelled "court" as "cort." Despite having left his own children and parents for the past eight years as he fled from justice, Stidham argued that his kids needed his wise guidance or they'd end up as drug abusers. He begged for the chance to help his elderly parents back in Arkansas.

By the time he began his prison time, nearly all of Stidham's partners in crime had completed their own sentences and been freed.

By fleeing to Black Canyon City, Hubert Stidham had followed in the bootprints of many an ex-con before him. Black Canyon City resident Lyle Mark Groves also had an interesting past. Once a dance-band drummer, he'd turned to robbing dry cleaning outlets in 1950s Detroit. During one robbery, he physically assaulted one employee and raped another. He later moved on to bank robbery, attracting the attention of federal authorities. Police officers set up a roadblock to nab him, but in a fairly comical series of events, Groves made off with a police officer's car and eluded capture. He drove to Florida, in the stolen car and rather than ditch it, continued to drive it to his job as a short-order cook at a Miami drive-in. It was the decision to keep the hot car that led to his arrest at the restaurant where he worked.

Held on a $25,000 bond, Groves was returned to Michigan to face charges. Upon conviction, he became prisoner #1507 of a total 1,545 prisoners ever to be committed to "The Rock" -

Alcatraz. Although Alcatraz history maintains no one was ever directly sent to The Rock, and had to "earn" their way their by misconduct at other penal institutions, Groves was sent there directly, checking in on May 31, 1961. His crime was listed as, "Bank robbery," on prison records and his papers clearly state, "Direct commitment."

After his release, Groves retired to Arizona. He lived, apparently well within the law, on Wagon Wheel Circle.

On July 18, 1989, Lyle Mark Groves passed away at age 66. His obituary gave no information about the sort of man he had been when young, nor what sort of man he matured into.

Aftermath and Author's Notes

In 1975, Catherine, Hubert Ray Stidham's wife since 1963, finally divorced him.

The Iron Cross Motorcycle Club is still active. The original Florida chapter founded by James "Big Jim" Nolan, though, was accepted into the Outlaws Motorcycle Club in the late 1960s. Nolan later was incarcerated in Arizona for charges related to the murder of John McQuillen. McQuillen was shot to death July 11, 1981 at The Bashful Bandit, an old, notorious biker bar on Speedway Boulevard, not far from where I once lived in Tucson. Nolan had been spending a lot of time in town trying to form an Outlaws chapter in the Tucson area.

In a minor but interesting coincidence, in 1939, another man named Purkhiser - an Oklahoma insurance executive named William Purkhiser - murdered a 13-year-old girl. Intending to murder the child's mother and stepfather, that Purkhiser found the girl home alone and bludgeoned her to death instead. I found no connection between the two Purkhisers other than the uncommon last name they shared and the unique circumstances of their crimes.

I was told the Midway Bar is locally famous for two things - the Filthy Five civic service group was formed there, and some guy once rode a horse inside. Originally it was Ellie's Frontier Saloon, owned by Leonora "Ellie" Strubhar, before Harold N. Gillum bought it. It's now called "Javalina Crossing."

Above: The original "Ellie's Frontier Saloon" sign, still in place in front of Javalina Crossing. Photo by the author.

I first heard the story of "Wild Bill Boady" and the bucking burros from René Faires. I relied on newspaper archives and public record to piece together the rest of his tale. I also used archives, public record, and Alcatraz historical sites in researching the case of Lyle Mark Groves.

The illustration at the beginning of this chapter is an original linocut print I did for this book.

Chapter 11

Dogs and Bodies

Bradley Funk, Don Bolles, and the Greyhound Track

Seventy-one year old Beulah Minter - all five-foot three of her - was a frequent visitor to the landfill southeast of Black Canyon City. There, Beulah and her husband, Roy, collected aluminum cans. Recycling outlets paid about 15 cents a pound in 1976 and the extra cash came in handy. At the time the landfill, not far from the VFW lodge, was unfenced. "It was two big holes," Sylvia McDonald told me. Whomever had the contract (T & H Construction company, that year) would push the new debris into them. The local kids, Sylvia among them, would shoot skunks at the landfill for sport. Sometimes, like Sylvia, they caught rattlesnakes there; once, Sylvia caught an albino rattler and kept it as a pet. Although to locals it was part of the regular stomping grounds, it seemed remote to city folks. Black Canyon was like that: just far enough away from the city that the urbanites felt they were in the middle of nowhere.

On Saturday, June 12th, Beulah was making her usual can-picking rounds in the summer heat, accompanied by her husband and Mary Herrell, when she found something much more significant. A charred body, hands and feet bound, had been dumped in the landfill. The victim had been shot five times in the back at close range at some other location, probably a day or two before, and then brought to Black Canyon for disposal. Such "execution style" murder indicates advance planning, maybe even professional involvement, maybe a link to organized crime. The body Beulah found was partially covered with trash. By chance, the T & H Construction company bulldozer was out of service when the body was dumped, or it would already have been covered with a layer of dirt and garbage. Perhaps the suspects responsible for the body's disposal counted on the daily landfill work to help cover their tracks.

A near-epidemic of newly-minted bodies turned up in Arizona in the mid-1970s. Bodies in the desert. Bodies on roadsides. Bodies in garages. Bodies in cars. Bodies in abandoned mine shafts. Bodies, mortally wounded, in emergency rooms. Bodies bound and burned in landfills. Bodies with uncanny connections to each other in a grim web, separated by just a degree or two of common ground. Black Canyon City, like New River just down the road, was a popular body-drop. Near enough to the I-17 freeway to make egress fast, easy, and innocuous, it was yet far enough from the metropolitan area to afford some seclusion while ridding oneself of the corpse and taking necessary measures to conceal the victim's identity and cause of death.

During the turbulent 1970s Arizona readers saw the same names in the papers on a near-daily basis: Sam Steiger. Don Bolles. Emprise. Bradley Funk. Neal Roberts. The Mafia. The Chicago Outfit. John Harvey Adamson. Kemper Marley. Ned Warren. They, too, were connected to each other. And they were indelibly, inextricably linked to a plethora of bodies.

The body dumped face-down in the Black Canyon landfill turned out to be 26-year-old Arab-American Hesham "Sam" Shehadi of 40 W. Georgia in Phoenix. The killers had gone out of their way to try to render the body unidentifiable, but they didn't incinerate him thoroughly enough to destroy his fingerprints. Shehadi's hands were amputated at the Yavapai County hospital and delivered to the Department of Public Safety in Phoenix for fingerprint examination. In Prescott, Dr. Philip Keen, the well-known Arizona medical examiner, was then working for Yavapai County and did the forensic examination of Shehadi's body. By the angle of the bullet wounds, he concluded Shehadi had been shot at least once while standing, the other bullets striking him after he was down.

Shehadi, a seedy transplant from Chicago, was a career criminal with a lengthy criminal history spanning three states, complete with an FBI number. Six-foot one, dark-eyed and dark-haired, Shehadi was a thief and a heroin user who'd done jail time in Chicago. Moving to Phoenix wasn't a fresh start for him; as an assistant manager at Earl Scheib's paint shop on Central Avenue, he helped himself to over $800 belonging to his employer. After returning to Chicago and being arrested, he was extradited to Phoenix to face charges in the theft. Certainly with his lifestyle he'd consorted with some nefarious characters and made some enemies. He'd spent a lot of time in recent months with a Phoenician named Robert Thomas Padilla - Bobby, to his acquaintances. Bobby and Sam both enjoyed flashy cars. Bobby Padilla drove a yellow 1972 Mercury Cougar. Sam had recently been seen in a 1972 Lincoln Continental. Bobby, about the same age as his friend Shehadi, shared the dead man's lifestyle choices, as well. A pimp and hustler with a fondness for drugs, Padilla was known as a fence for stolen goods.

By its timing alone, the discovery of Shehadi's body was immediately on the radar of the large force of detectives - and journalists - investigating the murder of reporter Don Bolles. Bolles, an investigative reporter for the *Arizona Republic*, had been headed to a meeting with a lead on June 2 when a bomb attached to his car was remotely detonated in the parking lot of the Hotel Clarendon at 401 W. Clarendon in Phoenix. He died of his injuries the very day after Beulah Minter reported Shehadi's body. The car-bomb death of Bolles was arguably the biggest Arizona news story of the 1970s. Its tentacles reached into the actions and pockets of politicians, businessmen, ranchers, small-time local low-lifes, and the dog-racing industry. Bolles, relatively unpopular with all of the above for his hard-driving investigations into Arizona corruption, had no deficit of enemies. His death, though, deeply impacted not only his friends and co-workers, but investigative reporters across the nation, bringing an impressive array of them to Phoenix for months to work on what became known as "The Arizona Project." The *Arizona Republic*, not only undaunted by Bolles' death and the implied threat to other reporters it brought, was emboldened. It put the fullest pressure of the press on organized crime and corrupt officials in Arizona, casting the brightest sunshine on the underworld in a truly heroic act of defiance.

Although police arrested John Harvey Adamson within three hours of Bolles' death, the list of suspects with direct involvement or guilty knowledge was already long - and growing. The corpse's proximity to the Black Canyon City Greyhound Track - just a few miles away on the other side of the freeway and north end of town - wasn't initially viewed as significant in any way. In fact, just as quickly as investigators considered a link between Shehadi's death and Bolles, they dismissed the connection. By June 16 they told the *Arizona Republic* "it is unlikely" a link existed. Too, the investigations were handled by entirely different agencies, with Yavapai County detectives Ed Mart and Ron Schutt, under the supervision of Chief Deputy Duane Kingsbury, spearheading the probe into the Shehadi death since the body was found in Yavapai County.

Thirty-two year-old John Harvey Adamson was a greyhound breeder. Six-foot one, dark-eyed and dark-haired, he too was a graduate of North High School, where he'd met his future bride, Saralou Combs. By college, Adamson was already known as something of a sadist to classmates at Arizona State University, active in hazing new fraternity members. Charles Kelley, a reporter for the *Arizona Republic* who did significant work reporting the Don Bolles investigation, described how as a member of the Maricopa County Sheriff's posse, Adamson kept his S&W .357 in his fraternity-house room; acquaintances described seeing him shooting a skunk at a Payson landfill with it and then, after the skunk was already dead, continuing to fill it with bullets in what they described as a "brutal" fashion. After marrying Saralou on August 23, 1966, Adamson - for a while a driver for Green Acres Mortuary in south Scottsdale — dropped out of college, never to return. Instead, he joined the military as a medic, and later, after his service, returned to driving ambulances for a while. He and Saralou ultimately divorced, remarried, and divorced again.

Just before the Bolles bombing, Adamson visited San Diego, accompanied by his girlfriend, Gail Owens. Gail owned La Strada, a restaurant at 3509 N. Central. At a hobby shop in San Diego, with Gail Owens along, Adamson purchased the radio receiver used to detonate the Bolles car bomb. There, too, lived a woman named Betty Richardson - a friend of Don Bolles and, not coincidentally, the ex-wife of a man well-known to Black Canyon City, Bradley Funk.

The Funk family had deep, old roots in Arizona. By 1911, the pioneer family owned a jewelry store on Washington Street in downtown Phoenix, not far from what would be the site of the first of their many dog tracks. The family began sponsoring and promoting sporting events, sponsoring a major-league softball team called the "Funk Jewels" and a bowling team called "Funk Jewelers" which played against teams such as "The Bacon Grille" and "General Auto Parts." The family also began their tradition of open-handedly contributing to local causes and coffers, a practice that made them popular among civic leaders and community members.

By 1942, the Funks were involved in organizing and promoting greyhound races at Phoenix Municipal Stadium. Their relationship with the dog racing community became contentious early on as they sought to control and profit from the fast-growing industry. David L. Funk - while a member of the Arizona Tax Commission, which until 1943 regulated dog racing - pressed dog meet coordinators to join him in organizing dog meets and to give him a 35% interest in the meets they were already setting up. In 1943, Funk was among several people sued by two members of the Arizona Kennel Club, J.P. Smith and Whitfield Brooke, who claimed Funk told them no permits for meets would be issued unless they worked with him and cut him in into their racing enterprise. The Tax Commission had also been collecting $100 per day in "supervisorial fees" which they justified as expenses for the commission members. In court, witnesses testified Funk told dog owners he controlled the Tax Commission and that no one but he and his brother, Arthur, would be issued permits to conduct races. Two other members of the commission, Thad Moore and Joe Hunt, had threatened to padlock the kennels and shut down racing unless the commission received the payments demanded for its members. Another member of the commission, D. C. O'Neil, was sued for his membership on the Tax Commission although he was not specifically accused of "wrongful acts."

As a result of the Tax Commission's greedy interference and underhanded dealings, in November, 1943, an Arizona Superior Court judge ruled the commission would no longer have any regulatory oversight over dog and horse racing beyond collecting 4% of the pari mutuel wagering pool. By then, Dave Funk was an ex-member of the commission, soon to be a leader in greyhound racing promotions in the state. Racing continued at both the Phoenix Municipal Stadium as well as at a 3/16th mile dog track at 17th Avenue and Roosevelt that had been converted from a midget auto-racing oval. The Funk family continued to operate their jewelry store in Phoenix. A "Help Wanted" classified ad in a 1943 edition of the *Arizona Republic* advertised for a "Colored girl or boy, janitor work, Funk's Jewelry."

By 1944, the Funk brothers opened the Phoenix Greyhound Park at the Roosevelt track. They continued their practice of wooing the community with civic-minded contributions and large advertising spreads in the *Arizona Republic*. One October 28, 1943 ad included a simple illustration of a running Greyhound, a sketch of an elegant grand entryway to the park, and the announcement "All gate proceeds for Arizona Society for Crippled Children ... Come out and help swell the proceeds for charity." The bottom of the ad noted, "Under State Supervision." Daily, the paper carried the results of the races.

In 1949 Brad L. Funk was a junior in the what was called the "Mid-Century Class" at North High School. Among his classmates were future Chicago Cub, Bill Denney, who'd grow into a valley radio personality and become the much-loved "Dean of Arizona Sportscasters;" and S. Portland "Port" Halle, who'd eventually own Wrangler's Roost resort in New River. One of Brad's friends, the slightly older George Harry Johnson, was a North High senior in 1946 who wore his ROTC uniform in his yearbook photos. Max Dunlap, a popular basketball player at North High, served as student body president in 1945. Dunlap, interested in farming and horses, developed a friendship with Kemper Marley, who'd become his mentor. One of Dunlap's classmates was future lawyer Neal Roberts, another of Brad Funk's friends.

As the greyhound industry grew in popularity and economic importance, so did the Funk's personal empire. They eventually owned six dog tracks in the state with locations in Tucson, Amado, Apache Junction, Phoenix, Yuma, and Black Canyon City. During the period from roughly 1968 to 1979, they brought in nearly $50 million in state tax revenue, primarily from taxes on wagering. Local papers - the beneficiary of many large and occasionally full-page ads by the Funks and their "Funk Racing Greyhound Circuit, Inc." - lauded the family. One full-page 1979 ad in the *Prescott Courier* described the family's "positive impact on sports, business, and community affairs."

By then, Don Bolles was long dead. Rumors of the family's link to his murder were familiar to investigators and the public. The family fought to preserve their reputation and popularity within the larger community by tightly controlling its image and promoting its good deeds in a variety of ways. Just as outlaw biker gangs coordinate toy runs, or stop to change tires for stranded motorists, whenever the Funk family seemed to feel the heat of public or official scrutiny, charitable events happened. When those charitable events happened, they reliably made it into the newspapers.

In 1967, the Funk family opened the Black Canyon Greyhound Park, operating it through a Delaware corporation called Western Racing, Inc. At the height of their success, they spared no expense in the design and construction of the grand and glossy stadium. Prominent Arizona architect Bennie Gonzalez, who also designed the St. Phillip de Benizi Catholic Church in Black Canyon City and the renowned Scottsdale Civic Center structures, designed the million-dollar building. Thirteen-hundred theatre-style seats and six-hundred table seats accommodated visitors who could dine on steak, lobster, chicken and shrimp while enjoying the view of the dogs running against a backdrop of the Bradshaw Mountains. Adults paid fifty cents admissions; children were invited to attend for free. The July 12, 1967 *Arizona Republic* proudly announced the grand opening.

In a convoluted business relationship, Funk Racing Greyhound Circuit, Inc., joined forces with a Buffalo, New York company called Emprise to run the thriving concession business at the family's tracks. By 1970 Emprise owned over 50% of five of the Funk's Arizona dog tracks as well as having interests in Arizona's smaller horse tracks. By then, dog and horse racing was supervised by the five-man Arizona Racing Commission. The commissioners retained questionable business relationships with racing operators; one commissioner, Donald Butler, was involved in land syndicates with dog track operators. In a May 13, 1970 article by none other than reporter Don Bolles, Donald Butler was quoted as saying he had to be in San Diego on the day the commission heard damning testimony about Emprise when meeting on whether or not to renew permits for the dog tracks.

When the bomb detonated beneath Don Bolles' car, despite the gravity of Don's mortal wounds, he was still conscious when help arrived. The words he uttered were clues to his murder: *John Adamson. Mafia. Emprise.*

In May, 1972, just shy of four years before Bolles would die, Brad Funk testified in Washington that Don Bolles, Congressman Sam Steiger, and Eugene Pulliam (publisher of the *Arizona Republic*) were conspiring to destroy his business. By then, the Funks, in partnership with Emprise, owned seven dog tracks and one horse track in Arizona. Funk, in retaliation, hired George Harry Johnson, one of his old North High School friends, to wiretap phones and collect dirt on his enemies, including Steiger and Bolles. He paid Johnson $15,000 to gather incriminating information. Funk also compiled an "enemies" list including names gathered from Funk employees.

Above left: John Harvey Adamson in his 1959 North High School yearbook photo. *Right:* George Harry Johnson in his 1946 North High School yearbook photo.

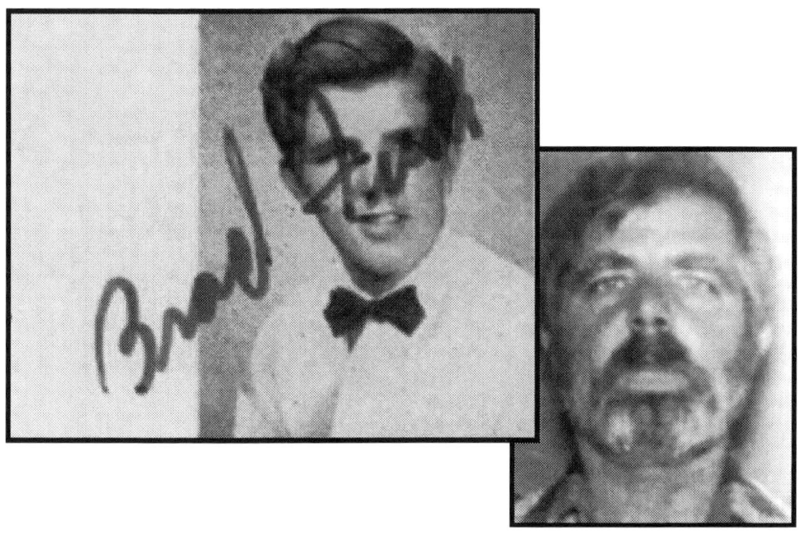

Above: Two faces of Brad Funk. Left, his North High School Yearbook photo, with his autograph.
Below: The long-empty Black Canyon Greyhound Park

The Bolles investigation was, for obvious reasons, elaborate, exhaustive and lengthy. Books - a series, in fact - could be written about the players, the evidence, the trial, and the aftermath. Those connected directly to the bombing were affiliated with a contingent of the Mafia known as "the Chicago Outfit," a branch of Chicago-based mobsters who also operated in Arizona. The mob had connections to Arizona's land swindlers such as Ned Warren (known as the "Godfather of Arizona Land Fraud); Ned Warren had connections to John Harvey Adamson; and so forth until an intricate and sinister web was spun. Meanwhile, gangland hits were responsible for a shocking number of killings in 1970s Arizona. Bodies piled up. Many were Mafiosi themselves; others, witnesses to hits; many seen as enemies to the mob. Allegations of official cover-ups related to the murders, from police brass to newspaper higher-ups to court officials and judges, were many.

Ultimately, in January, 1978, Max Dunlap and longtime bad guy James Robison, a valley plumber, were sentenced to death for Don Bolles' murder. Despite a series of related charges, mistrials, appeals, and innuendo, no one else was ever convicted. Dunlap's sentence was later reduced to life. Dunlap died in prison in July, 2009. Robison was acquitted on appeal in 1993. The death sentences didn't resolve the Bolles case and, in the minds of many, unjustly served to scapegoat two men who were very possibly patsies for the true responsible parties. Somehow, focus never rested heavily on the man whom many, including investigative journalist Don Devereux, believed to be guilty, and who had intimate alliances with so many people involved in the Bolles case: Brad Funk.

The Bolles murder remains to a large degree mysterious, and perhaps to many of us, officially unsolved. There's a good case to be made for Dunlap being a patsy; even Adamson, who admitted his involvement but once told his landlady he was but a patsy as well, wasn't the instigator. The powerful forces who masterminded the murder were never held accountable.

The Hesham Shehadi case was never solved. Through an extraordinary amount of research and follow-up to an equally impressive intuition, Don Devereux found multiple links between Shehadi and the Funk family. However, they remain shrouded in mystery and in conflicting statements by officials who investigated the case at the time. Devereux contended that local fence, pimp and drug dealer Bobby Padilla had possibly murdered Shehadi for motives relating to the Bolles murder and subsequent cover-up. Devereux's case is compelling. Again, insinuations of cover-ups and lack of communication between investigative entities plague the investigation.

Aftermath and Author's Notes

On May 24, 1978, nearly two years after Bolles' death, Phoenix attorney Neal Roberts was convicted of hiring John Harvey Adamson in a failed plot to blow up a federal building at 801 - 805 Indian School Road. Roberts' land development business, Orangewood Farms, was in negotiations to buy the building, which housed the U. S. Indian Health Services. His license to practice law in AZ was suspended. Roberts remained an object of suspicion until the end of his life in 1999 at age 66. Whatever guilty knowledge - or direct involvement - he had in the Bolles murder, he never revealed.

John Harvey Adamson served his twenty-year sentence at Arizona Department of Corrections as inmate #039025, released from the Florence prison on August 12, 1996. Adamson was ushered into the Federal Witness Protection program (WITSEC) and relocated to the east coast where, in May of 2002, he died under an assumed name.

Ned Warren, infamous "Godfather of Arizona Land Fraud," was convicted of fraud and bribery in 1977, his connections and payments to politicians, corrupt officials, and civic leaders having failed him at last. He died in prison in 1980.

Emprise Corporation later became "Delaware North," losing the name that at one time evoked images of organized crime and shady deals.

In 1982, the Black Canyon Greyhound Park shut down. For several years the building served as an indoor swap meet but for even longer it stood empty, abandoned and run-down. When I visited and photographed the site in 2016 and 2017, I walked carefully across a floor littered with used syringes and the detritus of derelicts. Graffiti marked the walls; jagged shards of broken glass from the enormous windows littered the floor.

The old grandstand in Black Canyon City is now gone, the site bladed. It was demolished in the spring of 2018. "It needed to go," locals said. Locals still wrangle the occasional question about an urban legend spawned by the internet a few years ago. The fictitious story claimed that in July, 1982, over 1,000 people were lethally poisoned at the Greyhound Park. This did not, of course, occur, and locals still tire of trying to convince the conspiracy-minded that no such thing happened, nor did officials engage in a cover-up of a mass casualty event. Those of us who've worked in law enforcement know there's no way government employees *could* keep such an event quiet.

Beulah Minter, lifelong resident of Black Canyon City, died in 1982 at age 77, survived by her husband, Roy, and their children.

Brad Funk died of a heart attack in 1989.

The people of Black Canyon City still remember the Funk family and speak appreciatively of their many contributions to the town.

Above: The Clarendon Hotel as it appears in 2018. To the left of the building is the parking lot where Don Bolles' car exploded. (Author photo)

I was 13 when Don Bolles was murdered. Although I never knew Bolles, as a teenaged Arizona native who wanted to be a writer, I felt his death deeply. Arizona was a smaller place, then, and we all felt closer bonds to events and people. I wrote Bolles a get-well card which, of course, he'd never live to read, but his family was thoughtful enough to write back personally to thank me for caring. I followed the story almost obsessively over the years; I think we all did. The murder, the ensuing investigation, and the light shed upon the deeply rooted corruption and mob activity impacted Arizona profoundly. Journalists from across the country congregated here to contribute to what became known as "the Arizona Project." One reporter, Don Devereaux, continued to investigate and document the Bolles case and related criminality for years after the others returned home or passed away. His website and blog were of great use in preparing this chapter.

I also extensively used newspaper archives, the North Valley High School yearbook, and official documents such as census records, military records, and vital records. My site visits to the long-abandoned Black Canyon Greyhound Park gave me a brief sense of what it had been like in its glory days; the setting of the track against the backdrop of the stunning Bradshaw Mountains must have dazzled visitors and dog owners hoping for their big payoff. Those dreams were built on a treacherous foundation. Other site visits included a trip to the Clarendon Hotel to pay brief homage to Don Bolles' memory.

Personal interviews touching upon content in this chapter included Sylvia McDonald; Rene Faires; and Bob Nilles.

The illustration at the beginning of this chapter is my original linocut block print.

Chapter 12

A Wounded Bridge

The Bridge Collapse of 1978

"I came here in November of 1978," Chuck Torrie recalls. "I should have known it was an omen because it snowed." Torrie, then a 34-year-old officer with the Highway Patrol, was assigned to Black Canyon City. The weather had been odd that year; in March, a foot of rain had fallen in a three-day period in the Bradshaw Mountains, causing flooding and a very swollen Agua Fria. In December the rains came again, and hard. By Monday, December 18, three days of non-stop rain had caused massive flooding throughout the state. Elsewhere in the nation, investigators excitedly closed in on serial killer John Wayne Gacy, and President Jimmy Carter struggled with protests and hemorrhoids, but Arizona contended with a deluge. Normally dry lands were saturated and unable to soak up anymore water. Small, seasonal creeks and formerly dry washes ran with more fury than the state's rivers usually do.

"It was my day off," Torrie says, recounting the tragic half hour before midnight. "I got a call from the volunteer fire department saying they needed help filling sand bags. I got in my jumpsuit and jumped in my patrol car. We had a CB radio in those cars. On the CB radio I hear this voice come over. It's a guy's voice. It says, 'The bridge is faltering.' I got on my DPS radio and asked if they had any reports of the bridge going down and they said no. I went across the old Black Canyon bridge. It was up and water was splashing over the edge but it wasn't flooded." The "old" bridge was on the main drag through town, and old portion of the Black Canyon Road, but the bridge the

stranger on the CB spoke of was the big, modern I-17 bridge built in 1964 over the Agua Fria, two miles south of the Bumble Bee exit. The bridge spanned 450 feet and had cost about $750,000 to build.

"I went to the dog track exit and came up southbound and there was a CTI truck stopped with the flashers on. There were two cars stopped with their flashers on but they were off the bridge. Everything seemed to be okay until I stepped out and as soon as I stepped out my knees started going like this because the bridge was going back and forth. When I got out there was this car, an El Camino or something that looked like an El Camino, and there was a dog in it, a poodle. There was an expansion joint and it was metal. There was an opening of about four or five feet with water running down. The other car I saw was on the other side and its flashers were on. The guy next to it was yelling but I couldn't hear him. I grabbed the edge and looked down and there was this woman. The force of the water was pinning her against the bridge. And she was screaming. You know how your mind doesn't work when you're under heavy stress? What seemed like a good idea at the time isn't? I thought I'd drive around to the other side and throw a tow rope to her. When I went to the other side, there was a guy there in a Cadillac. He said nothing seemed wrong but then as he was going off the edge of the bridge, everything dropped out from under him and the wheels - the running gear - got caught by the rising expansion joint metal and took the running gear off.

"I could see her over there. I put this cheek of my rump on the seat. I'm sitting, one foot on the ground and the other in the squad car, pushing the yellow button so I could get my tow rope out." Patrol cars were customized with in-dash trunk release buttons, the "yellow button" Torrie refers to.

"She was about twelve feet away. I was reaching to push that button and that whole road just in front of me just dropped. I just dropped it in reverse, hit the accelerator, and damn near hit that Cadillac or whatever it was he was driving. First of all, the river roaring with the big boulders that were bouncing off the bridge … and when that went in, it was a big *kawoosh*. The fastest I'd ever seen water going before that was down the toilet. These big boulders were suspended in the water and they hit the bridge They sounded like bombs going off. So anyway when that happened, I just called into dispatch and just told them, the whole damned bridge is gone.

"So what happened is the southbound side, the water raised that bridge up. When I did the accident investigation on this, what was the most probable that happened was the guy in the Cadillac was going, and then the vehicle that had the minister and the other people in it coming down from Prescott, and then she was behind that. The expansion joint on it was like this," Chuck puts his hands at an angle - "this being the ridge and this being the dirt, and the water started eating away the dirt. So it raised up and kept going. The second car with the minister and those people in it, the egress goes back like this, the second car goes into the mud. The water takes him and he's gone. She sees the sparks of the first car with no wheels. She stops and gets out to see where the first car went, and the bridge raised off the piers. It went up just like slow motion to me and then went down. Then the north side did the same thing."

As the bridge went down, the road crumbled on the banks. The little pick-up truck vanished, swept away by the river.

"When the bridge went down, and several hours afterward, the Highway Patrol helicopter came up because first of all we were looking for the car that went in with the woman in it. They dropped the medics off on the ground and put just me in the helicopter because I knew the area. We took off on the south side of the bridge off the freeway. And it was raining, pretty hard. We lifted up about 200 feet in the air and went around where the river wash was and by the time we went up by the dog track it was snowing. The pilot said we had to go down. The front of the helicopter was glass and the rotors were making snow flurries."

Above: The buckled bridge. Photo courtesy of Jerry Cannon.

"When we found the first vehicle, it was upside down with a portion of the tires - maybe eight inches or so - sticking out of the dirt. We tried to dig around it and there was too many rocks. When we finally got the backhoe and got him out, there was one black guy in there and I'll never forget it; he was light grey from being in the water.

Above and Below: The I-17 bridge over the Agua Fria at Black Canyon City that replaced the collapsed northbound bridge

"What I actually had was three different incidents. I had the one, where the Cadillac with the wheels off was, and then there was the second, with the car with all the people in it. And then there was the third with the woman who got out. We looked for her for days. And we went all the way down the Agua Fria to the juncture. I learned a lot in that thing. We found a mine shaft and it had one of the signs with the symbol for nuclear. I went in and suddenly heard pounding and then something ran across me. The damned javelina ran right across me.

"We got all the way around toward the Little Grand Canyon Ranch. We gave up our search there. We were walking. I'm 6'4" and there was debris above my head in the trees. The next day or so, someone had found her by the old school. The Portnovas owned it then. Just west of their main house, triangulated by where the old museum is. Upstream, up Black Canyon a bit. As you're walking down the river it was on the right side. That's where she was found." The "old museum" Torrie cites is the old Jeff Martin store and stage stop, now part of Rivers Edge RV park. By then, it was December 21st, three days after the disaster had occurred.

"She was half-clothed because she'd been tumbled down the river and she was buried in silt. They saw her hand first. We didn't find her, some civilians did. And that's when I called Yavapai County to come dig her out. She had to have gone under the freeway bridge and under the old Black Canyon bridge.

"The next day, we were out about three days with no sleep at all. Reynolds from the egg ranch was up by the bridge. He said when it happened he thought the damned Air Force was dropping bombs. I can see how he thought that because it was dark out. He thought they'd bombed the bridge!" Austin Reynolds wasn't the only local resident stunned by the noise.

Gary Chemas, living on nearby Palm Lane on the north side of the river at the time, recalls that the house shook when the bridge collapsed. Going outside to look, Chemas saw that the river - which moments before had been at his very feet - had dropped about six feet because of the bridge collapse. The debris from the downed bridges directed all the water to the other side of the river.

The woman Torrie had tried in vain to save was 40-year-old Geri Lee Griffith, driving from her home in Sedona to Phoenix with her little dog, Peppi, to pick her husband up at Sky Harbor Airport. Geri's calls for help were heard by the man who'd been a couple of cars ahead of her, Gordon Deming. Deming and his wife, Gladys, were on their way home to Phoenix after a family visit in Albuquerque. The Demings had lost their son in a December car accident seven years earlier. The circumstances of his death haunted Gladys on the rainy drive. She later told a reporter from the *Arizona Republic* she'd prayed for safety on the trip and that, in a prescient moment, she had packed a flashlight, pillows, and blankets.

Others had been praying that night as well. In the car directly behind the Deming vehicle was Pastor John Wesley Metzler from Scottsdale, accompanied by four fellow believers: Patricia Jean "Pat" Baker, 44, a clerk at Valley National bank; William Willeford, a 36-year-old mechanic; and two 20-year-old men who'd come to Phoenix out of state, Anthony Craig Webster of Detroit and Robert Glenn Webb from Thermal, California. The group had been attending a week-long Pentecostal prayer revival led by Metzler in Sedona. Metzler's wife remained at home in Scottsdale.

Just as Deming's Oldsmobile Toronado began across the bridge, the bridge began its collapse. The road ahead of the car buckled violently and began to break apart. Deming hit a concrete section of the bridge that had jutted upwards about a foot, flattening the tires and taking out the car's undercarriage. About 200 feet past the bridge, Deming was finally able to stop the car. Putting his flashers on and grabbing his flashlight, he hurried back to try to warn others not to cross the bridge. Pastor Metzler's car had already sailed into the raging river, landing on its roof. Geri Griffith stopped at the water's edge as she saw Metzler's car disappear and climbed out of her GMC Diablo pick-up, trying to make her way up the now steeply tilted bridge road but the water swept her away, pinning her in the position Torrie had found her, and ultimately carrying her downriver to her death.

The five occupants of the Metzler car were found within the wreckage of the car, a mile farther downstream of Griffith's pick-up. They'd died instantly due to neck and head trauma.

The bridge and six lives now gone, all that was left was debris and damage control. Newspaper reporters immediately began questioning the integrity of the bridge; state officials immediately began defending the design of the structure. Department of Transportation engineer, Sam Lanford, told the *Arizona Republic* the structure was not to blame, "it just gave way to nature." In February, two months after the disaster, Transportation Director W. A. Ordway maintained the bridge was properly designed for the peak flow of the Agua Fria. The design had even won a national award. Officials claimed a historic amount of flooding had occurred - over 60,000 cubic feet per second - well beyond the 37,000 cubic feet per second peak flow they'd planned for.

In fact, the December flow was about 25,500 cubic feet per second, according to USGS calculations. The bridge's piers had not been properly anchored to the bedrock below. The rip-rapping - boulders contained by heavy-gauge steel mesh - didn't extend high enough to protect the footing, and the March floods of that year had already been damaged. Damaged rip-rapping allowed the earth and gravel supporting the piers to wash away. Already "wounded" by previous flooding, the south piers failed during the 1978 flood. Bridge Engineer Jerry A. Cannon told me, "In my professional opinion, the footings on the bridge scoured out and were not resting on bedrock."

In January, a month after the bridge collapsed and before the debris had even been removed, the rains came again, falling over much of the state. The *Arizona Republic* said, "Perhaps the hardest hit by the rains was Black Canyon City." As the Agua Fria swelled over its banks, nearly 100 people were evacuated from the Grace O. Albins subdivision and the Hideaway Trailer Park as the town's streets flooded yet again.

The river wasn't - and isn't - finished threatening lives, homes, and bridges. The same flood that brought down the I-17 bridge also destroyed a bridge near Lake Pleasant. In 1980, another major bridge on the Agua Fria collapsed at Indian School Road. During a March, 1982, flood, a 29-year-old cowboy from the NO Ranch was riding home on horseback when he was thrown into the raging Agua Fria and drowned about eight miles southwest of Black Canyon City. The Highway Patrol helicopter again responded, finding Thomas Lester "Tom" Dent's body half a mile downstream. Tom's horse, unlike Geri Griffith's little dog Peppi, is said to have survived.

At five o'clock p.m. on Friday, May 23, 1980, the new bridge southbound over the Agua Fria opened. The northbound bridge opened two months later. With construction costing over $2 million, the bridges, supported by steel pilings extending 30 feet below ground, are wider and longer than those which collapsed. They are still intact.

Above: The Agua Fria during a 1935 flood. Photo from the Richinbar Mine Photo Collection, Arizona Geologic Survey.

Aftermath and Author's Notes

The Agua Fria flooding of November, 1978, echoed that of nearly sixty years before. On Friday, November 28, 1919, one of the Bradshaws - for whom the Bradshaw Mountains were named - told the *Arizona Republic* that a cloudburst opened over the Black Canyon. He described the cloudburst as so potent it resembled an ocean. The paper reported roads were washed out and boulders carried away and a vast amount of water racing down to the valley below. Just three years earlier a storm of similar force changed course of the river, uprooting trees and carrying soil, rocks, and other debris along. The river channel moved half a mile to the west during that flood. The Agua Fria had yet again remade itself.

The Agua Fria remains untamable. Massive winter rains in 2004 and 2010 again swelled the river well beyond its banks, inundating lower-lying parts of Black Canyon City, damaging and destroying homes, and causing evacuations. During a six-hour period in one 2004 flood, the river rose over 15 feet. The bridges have as yet held fast, but the course of the river is ever changing. As heavy rains hit, workers hasten to roads that cross washes and spray paint lines and numbers across the blacktop to mark the height of the water at specific times. Sometimes, the rains leave no blacktop to be painted.

I had the good fortune of interviewing Chuck Torrie for this chapter. Chuck's first-hand account of responding to the bridge collapse brought alive the tragic tale. Bridge engineer Mr. Jerry Cannon of Cannon Consultants, LLC, lent invaluable assistance in the form of expertise, bridge blueprints, and photographs. Others, such as Gary Chemas, offered first-hand recollections of the event.

I also relied on newspaper archives, primarily from *The Arizona Republic,* and official records. I made several site visits to inspect and photograph the site of the collapse as well as the bridges that replaced the fallen structure. I also visited the sites where Geri Lee Griffith's body was found and where her truck was located. After one recent heavy rainfall in which many roads in Black Canyon City were flooded, I toured the area, camera in hand, to study and photograph the havoc caused by the creeks and the Agua Fria.

The illustration at the beginning of this chapter is an original linocut block print I made depicting the rebuilt Agua Fria bridge in Black Canyon City.

Bilkes, Yee, 61
Biltmore Resort, 102
Biltmore Wonderbus, *102,* 103
Black Canyon, 61
Black Canyon City, 70, 103, 106, 116, 126, 129, 132 - 133, 145, 149 - 152, 157 - 158, 160 - 161, 164, 171, 175, *179,* 183, 186, 187
Black Canyon Creek, 25
Black Canyon Greyhound Park, 160, *167,* 173
Black Canyon Hill, 1, 13
Black Diamond Mine, 71 - 72, 74
Blakely, Monroe, 84
Blankenship, James William "Billy," 51
Blevins, Charles, 126, 139 - 140
Boady, Daddy Bill (see Hubert Ray Stidham)
Boady, Billy Ray (see Hubert Ray Stidham)
Bolles, Don, 157 - 161, 164 - 165, 168 - 170, 172 - 173
Bond, Sgt. Frank, 111 - 112, 129
Bond, June Evans, 112, 129
Boshears, David, 136 - 137
Bostwick, Johnny, 1
Bradshaw Mountains, 61, 115, 121, 165, 175, 185
Branaman, Elizabeth, 25
Branaman, John M., 25
Breakenridge, Billy, 13
Brooke and Linn's Plaza Feed and Sale Stable, 28
Brooke, Whitfield, 162
Broughall, Geneva, 133, 135
Broughall, James, 133
Broughall, Lawrence "Larry," 77, 131 - 137, 142
Brown, Amelia "Amy" (see Whitson, Amelia "Amy" Brown Marglin)
Brown, Archibald B. "Archie," 68 - 71
Brown, Irene, 70
Brown, Isabella, 70
Brown, Isabelle, 70
Brown, James, 75
Brown, John August, 67, 68, *69*
Brown, Margaret (see Raestle, Margaret)
Brown, Mary, 138
Brown, Robert, 75
Buckeye Road, 132
Bumblebee, 17 - 18, 62, 115, 176
Bunkhouse in the Bradshaws, 135
Burea, Jose, 51
Burleson, J. L., 71

Edgar, Milton "Uncle Miltie," 75
Edgar, Muriel, 75
Edgar, Nellie, 75
Ellie's Frontier Saloon, 154, *155*
Ellis, Harmon Lee, 140 - 141
Elmer Gantry, 101
El Porvenir, 62
Emprise Corporation, 158, 165, 170
Escondido CA, 75
Evans, John W., 30 - 31
Eyman, Frank, 112 - 114, 118, 124, 127
Faires, René, 155, 173
Ferdinand, Archduke Franz, 99
Field, Stephen J. (SCOTUS), 14
Filthy Five, 73, 154
Fimbres, Fermin, 3, 4
Findley, Jack, 121, 123
Fishback & Moore, 84
Fitch, Tim, 138
Fitzsimmons, Dr., 53
Five Points, 50
Flagstaff, 141
Florence, 114 - 115, 126, 135, 139 - 140, 142 - 143, 170
Flores, Catalina "Angel," 148, 150
Flores, Tito, 148
Four Winds Farm, 110, 122, 128 - 129
Foust, Mark "Angel," 136 - 138
Fraternal Order of Police (FOP), 127
Fremont, Governor John C., 3, 21
Fuhrman, John, 135
Fullajtar, Susan, 139
Fuller's earth (See Montmorillonite)
Funk, Arthur, 162
Funk, Bradley, 155, 158, 161, 163, 165, *167,* 168, 171
Funk, David, 162
Funk family, 161, 163, 169
Funk Jewels, 161
Funk Racing Greyhound Circuit, Inc., 164 - 165
Gabardi, Ralph, 141
Gable, Clark, 87
Gacy, John Wayne, 175
Gadd, William S., 137
Gaines, Bill, 139
Gallup (NM), 70, 99, 100, 101, 106